the Crafters
Companion

snowbooks

Proudly Published in 2006
by Snowbooks Ltd.
120 Pentonville Road
London
N1 9JN
Tel: 0207 837 6482
Fax: 0207 837 6348
info@snowbooks.com
www.snowbooks.com

The publishers have made every effort to ensure that the instructions in this book are accurate and complete. If you spot any errors or have any questions, please contact Snowbooks at crafterscompanion@snowbooks.com.

Why are things spelled differently? Because this book has contributors from all around the world, some people put in extra u's; others take them out. Hooray for diversity!

A catalogue record for this book is available from the British Library.

ISBN 1-905005-17-2
ISBN 13 978-1-905005-17-8

Contents

Introduction

When I set out to put together a craft book, I didn't want to create 'just' another collection of patterns. If that's all this edition had amounted to, I would have still been pleased just to work with the contributors, but I had something else in mind as well.

The question that crafters seem to face most often is 'why bother?' The query usually comes from our friends and relatives who happen not to craft, people who have never pondered the combination of corduroy and cotton, or felt and silk. But I think every crafter reaches a point where she asks herself this question, usually when she's half-way through a king-size patchwork made of 1" squares, or as the embroidery floss knots up for the umpteenth time.

As the back of this book wonders, why do we bother to make things by hand when we live in a world where our every material desire can be fulfilled by ready-made, shop-bought items? On the large scale, I like to think that the 'craft wave' is a reaction to this world; we create because the mass produced just isn't special enough. But if crafting is the desire for uniqueness, then the source of that must lie in every crafter – we must each have our own reasons for doing these things.

Well, yes and no. As I waited for the contributors to answer my questions, I sort of expected to wind up with half a dozen 'I was just crafty as a child'

responses (perhaps with a couple of 'I don't know's thrown in for good measure). And in a sense, that did happen. A lot of us were raised in creative families, and our instincts were encouraged every step of the way. But what we've done with those instincts, and what our creativity means to us now as adults – I think those aspects are special to each of us.

The projects in this book reflect that individuality. While our sources of inspiration often overlap, and certain influences like modern Japanese craft definitely tend to dominate, our interpretations can vary wildly. A skilled craftsperson may be able to reproduce each of these projects exactly, but a creative one won't be able to resist adding her own twist.

It has been a true joy to work with the contributors to this book. I 'know' them all in some capacity through the on-line journals we keep – a trend which has once again allowed crafting to be a team sport. Women used to gather together to knit and sew with their families and neighbourhood friends. For quite some time now, these have been solitary activities, perhaps because of their 'old fashioned' nature. Now we're recreating the networks we used to enjoy, and this time it's on a global level; that contributors from Australia, Britain, Portugal, and America can consider each other friends really is amazing.

So, I hope you have as much fun reading this book as I did creating it. It's been a labour of love, but if you're reading this, then it's finally finished, and I am one proud editor. When George Harrison was asked why he funded Monty Python's *The Life of Brian*, he reportedly said it was because he 'wanted to see it.' Similarly, I've managed the production of this book simply because I wanted to read it. I hope you'll agree it was worth the effort.

Anna Torborg (Editor)

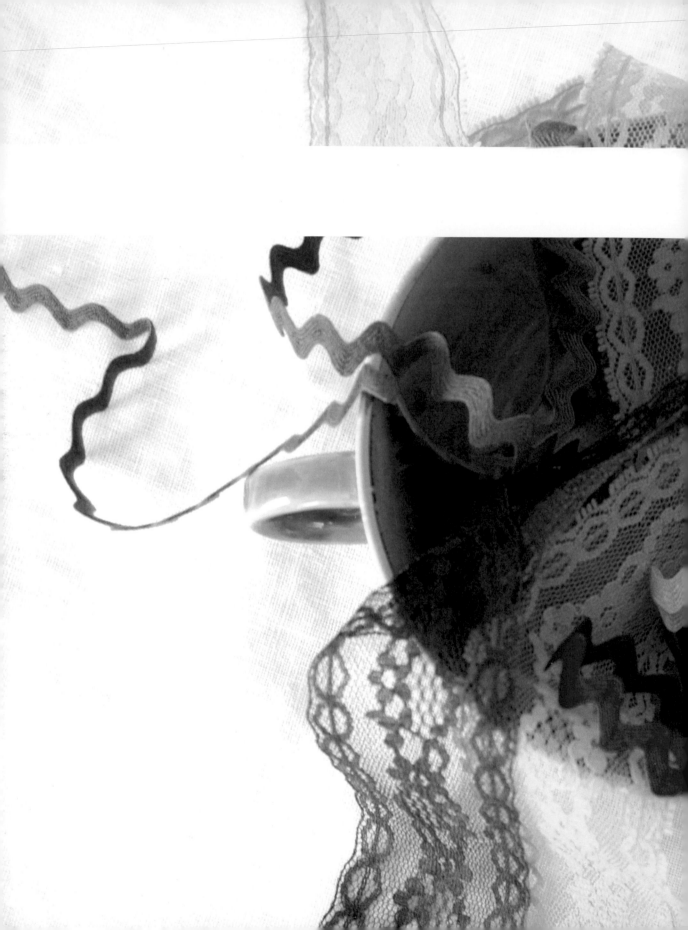

Crafters

Alison Brookbanks

Location: Sydney, Australia   Occupation: Architect   Age: 35

Areas of Interest: Knitting, Quilting, Textural Manipulation   Website: http://sixandahalfstitches.typepad.com/

why i create

Design is my life. I live it, breathe it, work it, and my life has always been filled with the chance to create. And crafting with different fibres is the perfect antidote at the end of a long day filled with steel and concrete. Through my crafting work I can express the design process which is often stifled by budget and programme constraints in my real life as an architect.

I grew up in a family that naturally veered towards the handmade – partly because of a lifestyle choice and partly because there was a belief that items could be made better, differently, cheaper and with more meaning than a store bought product. My mother constantly had a sewing machine out on the dining table. Material and patterns mingled with balls of wool and fair isle or aran sweaters half finished. My dolls slept in custom-made clothes and sheets, and I copied my mother with my own fully working miniature sewing machine. My father made us toys and dollhouses, and painted large abstracts layered in detail and texture. These memories ingrain themselves, become a part of you and lie dormant until one day you can rejoin the threads in the here and now.

The birth of my first child reawakened the need to create and produce handmade items for our house and our life. Somehow the pieces I made would prove my love for my child and cement the maternal relationship. It would reconnect me to my own childhood, and perhaps my child would grow up learning the values of handmade, creative play based on interaction and experimentation, using his imagination to fuel games and learning, rather than being drained by modern television and toys which overstimulate without allowing the child expression.

Baby clothes and children's items are soothing, filled with love and tolerant of fickle fashions. They are perfect in themselves – their smallness and exactness and the fact they represent new life, new hope and new dreams. It is the small, beautifully crafted

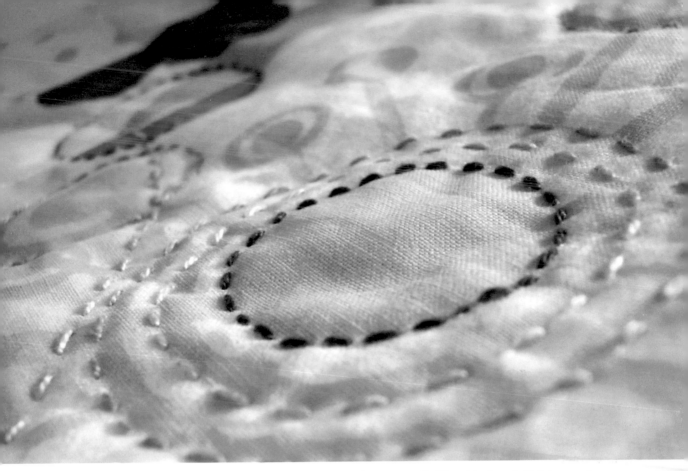

Opposite: 6.5st – The label under which Alison sells her creations.

Above: Details like this handstitching make a project really special.

I revel in the ability to find the perfect pieces to create a whole.

items which still appeal to me. They represent small vignettes – an idea which has constantly drawn me in all forms of design and particularly in architecture. I revel in the ability to find the perfect pieces to create a whole - whether that be buttons, ribbon, scraps of highly detailed fabric or the perfect knit texture. Each item works alone as a piece, but also gains new life when placed amongst others. Each stitch, knitted or sewn, each cut, each piece of fabric would have meaning and significance as part of a whole, and as an individual. Small things are quick, don't require as much patience, time or commitment as larger projects, and I find I often need the quick projects to satisfy my crafting needs rather than the long term projects.

The art world has always been a particularly strong influence on me, and I've achieved a lot by experimenting with different processes over the years. From time in a life drawing studio, to semesters spent etching and print making, to weekends spent painting, alternate forms of expression are important to me and my everyday life. I dream of a time in the future when I have space alone for multiple forms of crafting – printing, weaving, spinning, painting, sewing. I'd love to amalgamate all those into one form of craft somehow.

inspiration

I am most inspired when apparent simplicity can become something more complex by the detail, the proportion or the materials I choose to use. In the same way that Japanese origami is intrinsically simple and complex at once, it is these paradoxes I try to find in my own work. What looks simple can often be complex, and vice versa. I have learnt a lot from the Japanese way of doing things – the ritual of tea ceremonies mirroring the ritual of laying out and piecing together sewn patterns. The zen structuring of Japanese gardens echoing the proportions of material against material.

Strongest influences come from Japanese architecture past and present, which always seeks to find balance and calm against its surroundings, even with the use of apparently brutal materials such as concrete. There is a series of Japanese tea houses which I am particularly drawn to – haphazard weavings of bamboo slats which are textural, playful and when lit, strangely ethereal. Different fibre textures can have the same impact – the placement of an open weave like linen against a highly felted piece of knit can create drapes and folds amongst the fabrics which are far more appealing sometimes than the object they become. I love photographing my work to show these aspects of an object – that they are more than just a pouch, or an item of clothing, but can hold myriad shapes and forms which change with each pose.

The process of creating is an interesting one. Ideas germinate and become inspired to take shape. The most successful projects have been ones which demand my thinking time and which call incessantly to be done in eureka moments of insight. The idea gets thrown around in my head, developed, mapped out, constructed, studied, and pieced together,

This Page:
More stitching detail.

Opposite, Top:
Alison's basket bags are practical and attractive.

Opposite, Bottom:
Part of Alison's collection of inspiring ceramic pieces.

stitch by stitch, until it is an actual item floating in brain matter. Then I can sit and start making with absolute certainty. I have little time to prototype, tinker or think things through in real time, so when I start I can usually work through everything quickly. The quickness of a project is an important part of the process – I like quick fixes, instant results, and instant gratification. Yet I am a perfectionist, and I like well-crafted details and exactness of proportion combined with good quality materials. That last item is important – always buy the best you can, because it will show in your work and the way the pieces come together. I am learning through this crafting process that letting objects be themselves and working with the material can provide a better result than insisting on perfection in details. I bring to each item a well-balanced sense of proportion, colour, texture and visual display that always provides a whole – and intimate details within the whole. The pieces are three-dimensional in form and visual efficacy.

workspace

The dining table my mother used now acts as my studio table, embedding my own life and patterns into the grain of the wood. Littered around me

in my studio is ordered chaos. Perhaps it is more chaos than order, but everything has its place, no matter how haphazard that appears. Boxes of wool overflow alongside piles of material – each apparently unrelated and jumbled. But every single item has a purpose and a possibility. There is an idea in everything. Potential collaborations of wool and fabric form in groups around the room; pattern and craft books and magazines fall open to inspired images. They remind me what I am critically drawn to and are part of the stepping stone process of development. Projects in various stages of completion lie in a production line across my desk, the ironing board, the couch, and the floor. And in amongst that are little moments of pure design ethos – my growing collection of white and black ceramics, clear glass, small trinkets from fellow crafters and my own original artworks. This space represents control over my time, giving meaning to a sense of self which has changed through the amalgamation of motherhood and career woman. It's a space for me, where my value is absolute. It's a refuge from toys and cleaning and work, where my ideas can fall free and I can be selfish in what I do.

I don't consider myself a patternmaker – technically I am not trained in the art of cutting and sewing. I fall into designs, and let the material speak of how it wants to be used. My pieces are often very simple

in their construction, and I like that. There is often no need to be complex. Their complexity comes from their cut, or the fabric, or the combination of pieces. I like to take the same pattern and work it over many times, letting new life be born into it through changes of colour palette. The knitted pouch series that I have been working on recently is a great example of finding a simple form and, with subtle twists each time, achieving something fresh. The pattern included in this book takes the process one step further by adding in extra handmade items like shibori felting to make it truly unique. Numerous techniques can be incorporated within the structure, and this really appeals to my sense of wanting to achieve results quickly and easily.

This book is about a wonderful online crafting community, who have opened their doors and creativity to let people be inspired and let ideas flow and develop. Without the immense talent of these women, I would never have made some of the leaps I have. New worlds of texture, technique, ideas, form and shape, possibility and desire have been shown to me. To receive the feedback we do from others is a wonderful way to finish each project.

Below: Alison's desk.

Zakka-Style Pouch

Directions on Page 128

about the project

Combinations of texture, fibre, contrast colours and technique all join together in this deceptively simple drawstring pouch. Linen sits against fine cotton and shibori felt bands while a knitted bottom gives substance to the pouch. Bold sashiko embroidery gives the pouch a contemporary feel.

These pouches fascinate me, as there is no limit to the combinations of material and colour which can be incorporated into a small item. By keeping the colour scheme simple and limited to a white and red monochromatic scheme, you can add bold contrasts in the way of dark shibori felt and little feature buttons to give depth and texture. I have many uses for the pouches I make, from an unusual handbag, to a really portable way of carrying my knitting and sewing projects around.

Amy Karol

Location: Portland, Oregon   Occupation: Stay-at-Home Mom, Designer   Age: 33

Areas of Interest: Small Art Quilts, Abstract Wall Quilts, Design   Website: http://angrychicken.typepad.com/

why i create

As melodramatic as it sounds, I *have* to make things. I don't separate "art" and "craft" in my head, at least not anymore. There was a time right after college when I was really hung up on doing "serious art" which really wasn't serious at all, but was "art" in the sense that it wasn't crafty and was represented by galleries and participated in juried shows. I guess if I were to differentiate between art and craft now, it would only be that craft often has a utilitarian purpose or history, but that's about it for me.

Back then, I would feel guilty for crafting, but when my natural interest began to shift towards crafting even more, I really just let all of my hang-ups go. I craft as a result of my circumstances. I have an interest and experience in painting, digital video and film, along with music and performance art, but these mediums aren't very practical when I'm at home with my daughters full time, so I do what I can, and what fits in my life. Right now, it's primarily sewing, drawing and working on my craft blog.

The art/craft debate ended for me when I realized that I felt the same doing both, so it didn't really matter what I was doing; as long as I achieved that feeling, I was happy. When I work, I have no concept of time. I can just be 100% absorbed in what I am doing, and I think it's the only time of the day I am not multi-tasking. This brain/hand connection is meditative for me and is really what keeps me going. The worst times in my life, looking back on it now, have come from when I wasn't able to — physically or emotionally — be creative. That's why I don't know how to answer the question "where do you find the time to do so much?" which I hear a lot. It's like asking me how I have time to sleep or eat food. I just do.

My mom says I have always been this way. She started calling me "craft queen" when I was about three, and the nickname still comes up, embarrassingly. When I was young, creating was such a wonderful experience for me, because I could do it alone; it didn't require other friends. There were only boys in our neighborhood when I was growing up, and I had a brother, so I learned ways to keep myself busy by myself, and crafting was the main one.

Conversely, I think creating is also a way I connect to other people, especially other artists and crafters. At this time in my life, it's so hard to have a real connection with people other than my family. I am in my early 30s, and all of our friends have jobs, families, marriages and very full lives; there isn't a lot of free time. When I do connect with people, it's usually about the kids. This is great, but it's hard, because I am with the girls all day. The craft blog has kept me connected to what others are doing and gives me a way to contribute to the big show-and-tell. This has been so important for me as an artist. Not just to get feedback, but to feed me visually as well. The only thing I need to be careful of is being online too much and knowing when to turn off the computer and put my head down and work. I have been able to surround myself with friends online who would never think it's odd for me to spend so much time writing and thinking about iron-on vinyl or which thread I sew with. This connection

When I work, I have no concept of time.

Opposite: "Location Device" – Monoprint and collage on paper.

Below: Detail of small quilt "Spotsy."

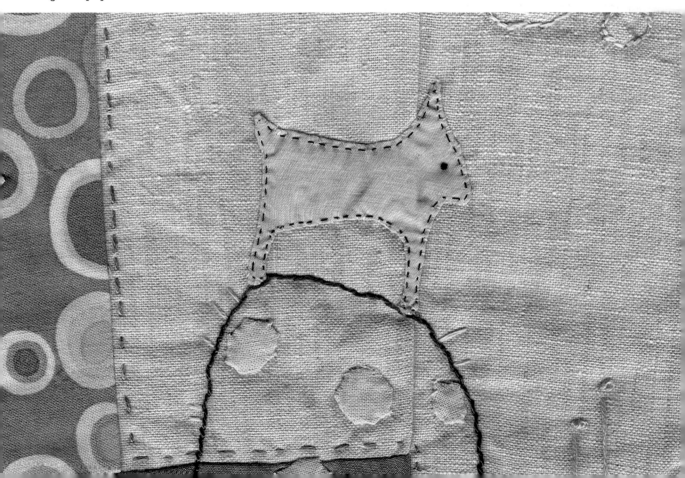

has really affected my creative output. I know without the encouragement and enthusiasm of the community online I would never be doing so much. It feeds itself and I think this is such a wonderful thing. I feel like I am really participating in life when I create, not watching it go by.

inspiration

I am inspired by so many things. My tastes change, like everything, but right now they're quite eclectic. I've always liked mid-century graphics, textiles and furniture, but lately I have been much more excited by 19th century graphics, like old Sears catalogs from the mid 1800s, old cookbooks, and periodicals. I love music and the radio, especially talk radio, like *This American Life* and other public radio shows; listening when I work is very inspiring.

Also, anything domestic – as in for the home – is really fascinating to me, especially when its roots are utilitarian but the execution makes it art. Like quilting. I feel such a connection with women who made quilts to keep their families warm. That was the real purpose of some of the quilts, but the women also made choices about fabrics, placement, color and design, and I love making the same decisions, even though my quilts look nothing like the historical ones that I am so in awe of. Aprons also get me especially excited, because I love thinking that so much time was taken to make a garment that was going to get so dirty. We would never do that today. Well, we don't do that, do we? We don't sew aprons today. We all use paper towels and throw them out.

I have also been researching needlework more, especially samplers. I think this interest is due to my two girls and wanting to get them started on hand sewing pretty soon. I also love the family tree and historical documenting that happens in needlework, like births, deaths, willow trees, and all the life and death imagery associated with those things. The morbid beauty is really amazing to me.

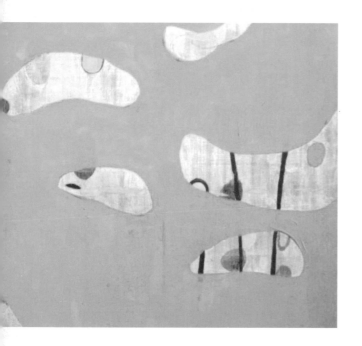

Above: Detail from one of Amy's abstract quilts.

Left: 'Fresh', acrylic on canvas.

Opposite: We all like to pretend our studios are always spotless, but Amy doesn't have any qualms about showing her space as-is.

workspace

For about five years I had a studio outside of my home, and I would spend all day there. I can barely remember that now. Since we bought a house and had the girls, I have moved around in various corners of our fluorescent-lit basement. It is finished, with carpet and all, but it's far from ideal. Half of it is a play area and half of it is my space. There is no natural light and a ridiculously large portion of my storage is on the floor.

One thing I love about my space is my ability to work in it with my children. Although having alone time is important to me, I am reminded daily of my earliest craft memories when I see my girls playing with thread, pins, scissors and other notions, which are, no doubt, totally dangerous and inappropriate for them to be playing with. My mom's own craft room was never off limits to me, and apart from not using the fabric scissors for paper, I could use anything in there. I know this is what made my first experiences in crafting so amazing. I was never told no, and I know I developed my early skills because of it. So, when I watch my two year old take all the stuffing out of a bag for the tenth time in an hour, I just smile and leave it on the floor until naptime.

Quilted Throw

Directions on Page 130

about the project

The organic, unplanned process of making this quilt, "Yellow and White", is where I feel most comfortable with textile work right now. When I paint on canvas, I work with paint, drawn lines, and collaged paper. All these elements I now use in my quilts, but with fabric and thread instead of paint, paper, and pen and ink.

When I work on these large quilts, I really do very little differently than I do when I paint. I work on the wall, with a piece of flannel tacked over the wall surface that the fabrics stick to, and I compose as I go and never know what the quilt will look like until it's done.

Because I work this way directions are hard to give. I can give you directions on how to make a quilt that looks really similar to this one, but the exact number of shapes or the exact sizes of all the background pieces are not given, simply because it would be so tedious for you to recreate it in this way. It's more of a "style" of working with fabric that I am showing here rather than an exact pattern. So have fun and don't worry about making it perfect.

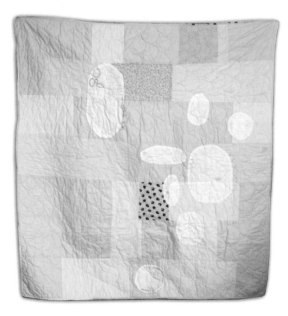

Anna Torborg

Location: London, England   **Occupation:** Publisher   **Age:** 25

Areas of Interest: Bags, Quilts, Printing, Crochet   **Website:** http://www.twelve22.org/

why i create

When I think about my craftiness, it seems like there's an unbroken link from now back to my childhood. In truth, there was a period in which I wasn't that interested in crafty pursuits; I was absorbed in other activities. Even though my childhood days were spent painting ceramic figurines and cutting out paper ponies, the crafting I now indulge in wasn't necessarily born from those activities. So how did I get to this point?

One day I made a hamster. That's not possible, you say, only God can make a hamster, or maybe a mommy and a daddy hamster, if they love each other very much. But one day I went into my local craft superstore and decided I was going to make my own rodent friend. Technically, I already had one – this was when I was at university, and Monty was my personal mascot, a particularly tame and friendly golden hamster buddy. The cartoons I'd drawn of him had inspired me to go 3D, and this was when it all started. That was the turning point.

What do you need to make a hamster? Well, you should look for felt, some thread, string for the arms and legs, and some stuffing. And then you just start creating. Even though I'd played around on my mother's sewing machine when I was younger, hand sewing this fellow was tricky. I could visualize the basic shapes I would need to get the finished product, but perfecting them was entirely down to trial and error. In the end, my hamster had the head

from one prototype and the body from another, but he was still perfect.

It was around this time, when I was becoming the Frankenstein of the toy world, that I discovered Craftster (www.craftster.org). Here was a group of people who were proud of their creations – they shared their ideas and showed off their finished products, and there was hardly a hint of embarrassment! Wow. I certainly wasn't running to show my friends the silly animals I'd made, but maybe these Craftster people would understand. Posting to those message boards gave me my first taste of approval and praise for this new creativity, so I took it to my blog.

I began keeping an on-line journal nearly six years ago, which isn't eons (even for the internet), but it was well before your average person would have known what a blog was. Looking back, I'm not sure what I wrote about before I started crafting. But a slow trickle of comments grew steadily as more and more craft blogs popped up, and soon I was part of an amazing community.

The support and inspiration I'm given from this network has allowed my crafting to grow by leaps and bounds. From the first tote I made a few years ago to the more impressive (I hope!) bags I make today, I'm always amazed to find that this is something I'm really learning. It's not something

I'm always amazed to find that this is something I'm learning.

Opposite: The hamster that started it all.

Below: Detail of Anna's lunch bag.

I study in the traditional sense, but practice really does make perfect. I'm always pleased when I think of the skills I have today that didn't exist in me a mere four years ago.

I love crafting because it is such a broad term. I began with a felt hamster, but I now sew, draw, quilt, crochet and knit, and I print with both my letterpress and from hand-carved stamps. I do these each with varying degrees of skill, but I enjoy them all.

Crafting, for me, is about turning an idea into reality. I really admire my friends who can say they appreciate each step of the process, but that's not true of me. I like to develop an idea, but I find cutting fabric a bore, ironing is hot and tedious, and sewing can be frustrating and never-ending. Each step closer to being finished is exciting, though – I love watching my progress, especially in large projects. Seeing the end product and knowing I made it – that is creative heaven.

Above: A patchwork strip bag.

Below: Very pink bird prints.

inspiration

My tastes really vary and evolve from moment to moment, and it has to be down to the variety of sources from which I take inspiration. Perhaps the most obvious of these sources is the vast quantity of magazines I buy each month. I'm sure there are people out there with upwards of twenty magazine subscriptions, but I haven't got a single one. I enjoy my trips to the book shop too much to subscribe; I don't care if I have to wait an extra day or spend an extra pound – waiting for a new issue to appear on the shelf is part of the excitement.

I have a number of magazines which I buy regularly, and rather than being craft magazines, they're all of the 'home and garden' variety. I love to see photographs of carefully (and sometimes not!) decorated rooms and see how everything fits together. I find that the aesthetic of a room can inspire a project by itself. Instead of saving all the magazines I buy, I clip my favourite pictures and paste them into an inspiration book. The book's primary purpose is to give me decorating ideas for my own home, but the colours and styles often inform my crafting choices.

Speaking of that, I find that I'm drawn to a surprising array of different styles. I feel like my brain is a Venn diagram, where each circle is a unique style – making the circles overlap is definitely a challenge. I love the modern Japanese style which has taken over the craft world, but I equally adore the clean, bold Scandinavian look. I use a lot of Kaffe Fassett fabrics, and am very prone to going overboard in the print department. I'm fond of the pinks and aquas of shabby chic. And I love retro prints, anything from the 30s to the 70s. How's a girl supposed to decide between all those?

One of my favourite aspects of the internet craft community is that we're so happy to be each other's inspiration. It's not so much the finished projects which inspire me, though they can certainly be fabulous. I tend to see the combinations of fabrics and colour. The best example of this is the number of projects I'd been seeing in reds and yellows and blacks. This isn't a combination I would have been drawn to myself – not so much because I wouldn't have thought of it (which is sometimes true!), but because I simply thought I wouldn't like it. But the colour mix grew on me, and when I started choosing patterns for a new quilt, what was I drawn to? Exactly. I love the finished product, and in a sense, I couldn't have done it alone.

Below: A favourite quilt in surprising colours.

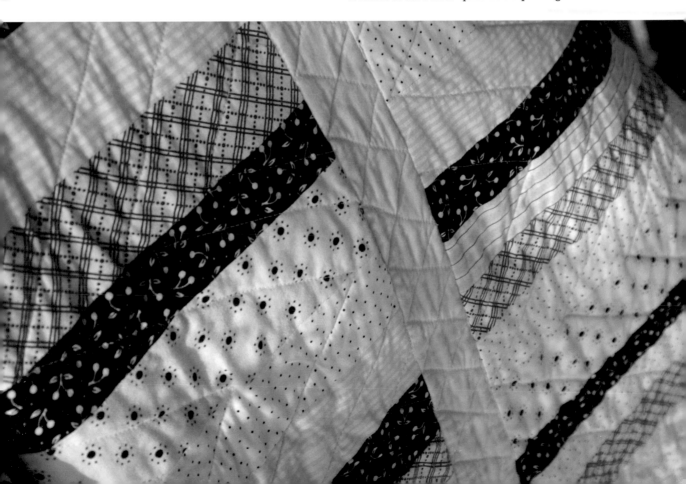

workspace

When I finished that first hamster, I put the left over materials in a shoebox, and that was the extent of my 'studio'. But crafting is an excellent hobby for hoarders, and it wasn't long before the shoebox expanded to a set of drawers. I lived in a studio apartment for a while, and its tiny dining room became the craft room as my obsession grew. It was great to spread out my mess on the table and walk away mid project without worrying that it would be in the way.

When I moved to London, I packed three bags, and two of them were filled with fabric and notions – there was one for clothes, and everything else would just have to wait! It was symbolic of crafting's hold on me; the thought of having to go a day without a project was frightening.

I've moved house once again since arriving in London, and for the first time, I have a proper room all to myself for my studio – with a door and everything! I have a large desk which holds both my computer and my sewing machine. I've got several cabinets which hold boxes of ribbons and trays of my letterpress type, and all my fabric is kept on shelves in the built-in wardrobe. My view is spectacular, and I have to remind myself to

appreciate this luxury while it lasts – my studio is just about perfect at the moment.

In a sense, decorating or designing a studio can be difficult, because it's a space that's just about you. It sounds great, but when you're drawn to so many different styles, it can be a challenge to keep it toned down, especially in a small space. I'm always amazed that my studio does seem to 'hang together,' given that the individual pieces can be quite disparate. I've got stark Scandinavian prints and frilly tea towels and modern storage, but I think it somehow all works.

Having started with a shoebox, I know I don't really need the dedicated space to create, but it's lovely to escape into my own room and sit amongst the fabric and ribbons and dream.

This Page: Anna's sunny studio.

Opposite: A very girly little purse.

Market Bag

Directions on Page 132

about the project

After realizing how much of my food went off before I got around to eating it, I decided to make an effort to change the way I shopped. Instead of buying the week's groceries in one go, I would visit the supermarket a few times a week and buy only what I needed for the next couple of days. It's a great idea and definitely reduces the amount of food that goes to waste, but I don't like the piles of plastic carrier bags that can build with this scheme. So I decided to solve that problem too.

This market bag is great and versatile. It's roomy and strong enough to carry your cartons of milk, and it cinches up at the top to make sure the biscuits don't go rolling away. Best of all, it has a handy pocket inside which the entire bag can tuck into. I can carry this around in my regular purse, and I've always got an extra bag ready to go.

My bag is made from light weight cotton, for maximum foldability, but there are many variations to try out. Construct yours out of canvas for a rough-and-ready version, or line it with a waterproof fabric for carrying cold items. You can even simplify this already easy pattern by leaving out the pocket and cinch, and you'll have a bag you can whip up in no time flat!

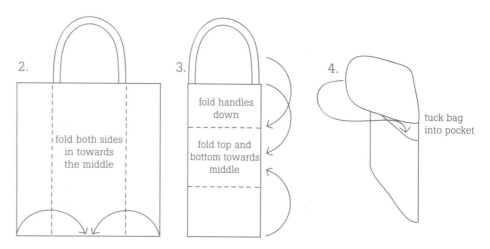

1.
turn pocket out of bag and free from handles, turn pocket inside out

2.
fold both sides in towards the middle

3.
fold handles down

fold top and bottom towards middle

4.
tuck bag into pocket

Cassi Griffin

Location: Hailey, Idaho   **Occupation:** Stay at Home, Homeschooling Mom   **Age:** 45

Areas of Interest: Pincushions, Totes, Soft Toys, Decorations   **Website:** http://belladia.typepad.com/

why i create

I've been crafty all my life. My mother and grandmothers were all talented at a variety of crafts and needlework, so making things just seemed to come naturally for me. I can still hear my grandmother say, "Well, I can make that," whenever we would go out shopping and I'd show a special interest in something. As kids, my twin sister and I indulged in every sort of crafting possible from bath salts to book making, from weaving to wood burning. We were also entrepreneurially minded when it came to our crafting; among other things, we made puppet kits and sold them door to door to our very generous neighbors!   Little did I know that that would be a career path later in my life.

I wanted to be like the pioneers and make candles and rag rugs and corn husk dolls. I loved books like the *Little House* series and *The Boxcar Children*, and movies like *The Swiss Family Robinson* and even the TV series *Gilligan's Island*.   My imagination would be all fluttery thinking of making cups from coconuts and digging through the local dump to find cracked china for dinner plates. That type of thinking has always been the cornerstone of my personal style; for example, if I need new curtains, then my first thought is to check my vintage linen collection to see what I can make rather than look through a catalog or go to the mall.

I'm raising three kids on my own, and since we home school, my days are very busy. I'm like most

people and don't really enjoy housework, but I think what I least like about it is that you never have much to show for your labor. The laundry, the meals, the grocery shopping, etc. are just a never-ending cycle, and it's hard to feel any sense of accomplishment when it never seems to be done. When I craft I end up with something tangible. I have something that says, "Look what I did!"

I love the challenge of seeing what I can create on my own, and when I'm pleased with the result it's extremely satisfying. If other people like what I make too, then that is just icing on the cake. I am mostly self-taught and my work improves through trial and error – and patience! When I was younger, I crafted mostly for the end result; sewing was one of my least liked crafts because there was so much prep work. I hated cutting out the pattern, all the pinning, and the threading of the sewing machine – I just wanted to get it done and enjoy my creation. Now, I enjoy the process as much as I do the end result. These days, sewing has become one of my favorite activities. I love the smell of the fabric the first time it's ironed, matching the thread, aligning the pattern pieces, and pressing open the seams. As far as hand sewing, I find it almost meditative. I enjoy sitting in the evening with my work in my lap and my hot tea nearby and letting my thoughts drift. I don't like to make mistakes, but when I do I don't get nearly as frustrated as I did when I was younger. If I make a mistake, I pull out the stitches and redo them, because I know I won't be happy with it if I don't. It's all just part of the process. Crocheting is also very relaxing for me and I find the stitch repetitions are like the chanting of a Buddhist monk, allowing the dust of a stressful day to settle.

The things that I have that are most special to me are things that were handmade by my family. A quilt from my great-grandmother, handmade baby clothes from my grandmother, a sculpture from my mother, drawings by my sister, and of course first drawings and pinch pots from my children. These are the things that I hold most dear – all handmade, all from the heart.

I love the challenge of seeing what I can create on my own.

Opposite: Business cards for Bella Dia, Cassi's design label.

Below: Crafts, notions, and inspiration on Cassi's craft cabinet.

inspiration

If my inspiration had a theme song, it would be *What a Wonderful World* by Louis Armstrong. I truly find inspiration all around me, but especially in nature. I'm lucky to live in a beautiful rural area where I'm surrounded by forests and rivers, snowy mountaintops and bright blue skies. I get to experience all the lovely shades and shapes of nature right outside my door. I am captivated by the subtle color changes at dusk and the way the light at different times of the year plays up the variety of tones in familiar objects. Although we are covered up in snow for six months of the year, spring and summer are vivid with brightly blooming wildflowers. My gardens are mainly perennials and it's just one more place where I can see the shift of color and light as the seasons come and go.

My mother and sister and I used to own a flower shop, where I learned about many different types of flowers and greenery. My experience as a floral designer has been a huge influence on my designs, especially the pincushions. I usually have a flower in mind when I'm creating one from felt or I'm embroidering; I'm trying to get the feel of the flower and am not interested in reproducing it. Flowers alone supply an endless source of ideas for shape and color.

Children's literature is another vast source of inspiration for me. I have a rather large collection of children's picture books and I love perusing through them when I need to spark my creativity. Some of my favorite illustrators are Feodor Rojankovsky, Demi, Elsa Beskow, Peter Sis, Wanda Gag, Lois Lenski, Esther Wilkins, and Garth Williams to name a few. A favorite pastime is looking at books in the children's section of used bookstores and finding new treasures to bring home.

I developed an early love of all things vintage from going to flea markets with my mother and grandmother. My grandmother was a huge antique collector and her house was like a museum in itself, so it was a great place to let your imagination run rampant and see design from other decades. In the same way, period films are another great source of inspiration. I especially love looking in the background of scenes to see how the room is decorated, what toiletry items are out on the vanity, color combinations, architecture, clothing, and so on.

Inspiration for me is just a way of looking at the world and reinterpreting what I see into something tangible. Images rain down like confetti and I go around picking up the little colored pieces and try to make something pretty! I'm aware of trends but I don't put much consideration towards them when I'm designing new items. Being in my forties, I'm only too well aware that trends come and go but good design stays constant.

Left: Cassi's sewing machine, waiting patiently.

Opposite: Fabric, valuable fabric.

workspace

It would be lovely to have a dedicated room for my crafting but that's not possible right now. Since we home school, the extra room we have is used as our schoolroom, so my work has taken over the kitchen and dining room and most other flat surfaces nearby. I've tried to convince the kids that we can do without the kitchen but I haven't gotten very far with that idea. I have several old cupboards that are stuffed with fabric and ribbon and assorted other do-dahs and I'm always on the lookout for vintage canisters and old wooden boxes because I use them for more storage space. If you look in almost any lidded container near my workspace you will find it stuffed with something that I use in my crafting. I have several wire mesh carts that I've organized with my sewing necessities and I pull those around with me depending where I'm doing my work. The sewing machine is on the kitchen counter and the iron is always up; having things out and accessible makes it a lot easier to get crafting done but it's not the way to have a clean house!

Fabric Scarf and Brooch

Directions on Page 134

about the project

This is the perfect project for a sewing novice, but the finished product is amazingly versatile and fun. Because these scarves are so quick and easy to whip up, you can make an entire range to match your wardrobe, in weights to take you from cool autumn evenings to the coldest winter days.

The pretty flower brooch can be used to fasten the scarf in place, and it's a lovely accessory all on its own! Because this project uses a relatively large piece of fabric, it's ideal for showcasing a print you can't bear to cut into pieces.

Fiona Dalton

Location: Adelaide, Australia   Occupation: Stay-at-Home Mum, Graphic Designer   Age: 33

Areas of Interest: Soft Toys, Bags, Children's Clothes   Website: http://hopskipjump.typepad.com/

why i create

The impulse to make things has always been with me. My mother is a painter and crafter and so always encouraged my brother and I to make things and engage ourselves creatively. I think I must have been a bit obsessive and single-minded about craft as a kid, because one of my earliest crafting memories is badgering my parents to buy potters clay and, once it was purchased, asking them to bring it out to play with over and over and OVER again. I littered my poor parents' house with those ugly clay creations. I'm still obsessive about the things I make, but I'm glad to report that I can unpack my own equipment now. And I even clean up after myself sometimes, too!

As long as I can remember, craft of some sort has been a part of my life - from paper crafts such as making Christmas cards and invitations, to sewing bags and cushions, baking cakes and restoring furniture (with mixed results for the latter, I might add). Why do I do this when I could just head to a department store for a similar item? These are my two cents:

1. There is a significant sense of personal satisfaction, a sort of self administered pat-on-the-back, one gets from completing a project and standing back to admire the results of one's handiwork;

2. Home-made has more personality, more meaning and is more from the heart than store-bought things;

3. Crafting connects us to some of the charming bits of times past;

4. The process of making things often seems to have a meditative, calming and even healing effect.

Like most people who make things, I find crafting immensely satisfying. My husband always teases me for 'going about the long way' to achieve something. The production of our wedding invitations, for example, involved two separately printed sheets, ribbons, glue, stamps, a wax seal, and lots of folding, cutting, and gluing. In other words, lots of time.

Opposite: Detail from a baby's quilt.

Above: Fiona's soft toys are a hit with both children and adults!

I love the challenge and thrill of perfecting a new skill.

All before we wrote on them and addressed the envelopes. To me, this is part of the fun of celebrating an occasion. Handmade details can make an event unique, more personal and - yes - just the way I like it. Perhaps there is an inner control-freak inside every crafter? In any case, for me it is every bit worth the extra 'trouble' to see an idea come to fruition.

Similarly, I love the challenge and thrill of perfecting a new skill. They are usually small things, but the conquering of a crafting goal can have enormous feel-good mileage!

The second point – that hand made is much nicer – is a slippery one, so much dependent on personal taste, fashion and aesthetic. Remember all those unattractive woven hard-baked bread wall hangings and gumnut-people crafted in the 1980's? I know that some of the things we make now will suffer a similar fate; craft is as much driven by fashion as anything else. However, at their best, hand-crafted items seem to have special powers. A friend of mine has a baby blanket that was knitted by her great grandmother. It was used to receive all her great grandmother's babies, and those of her grandmother and aunts. Even my friend was bought home from hospital wrapped in it. When I visited her a few weeks before the birth of her first child last year, she had the blanket laid out, waiting. We stared at it with reverence. Sure, any blanket that plays that kind of starring role in a family is special, but the fact that this one was hand knit by my friend's great-grandmother added to its importance.

For most of us, time is a very precious commodity; it is so nice to receive something that someone has poured some of hers into. Knowing that she's probably spent that time thinking of you and what you might like to receive makes it extra special. When an e-mail is the norm, there is such charm in receiving a hand made gift or card.

Thirdly, I also love how crafting can connect us to the past. My mum taught me how to sew, and my grandmother taught me how to knit and bake. I sew with a reasonable amount of recycled fabric: fabric from charity shops or cut up old clothes. I do this because I like the patterns I find in older fabric, as

well as the quality of some of the material, especially wools and tweeds. Thrifting is also needed because we are budget conscious, and it's important for me to not let my sewing supply purchases get in the way of necessary things like groceries or health care! I love being able to create something from an item someone no longer wanted. But most importantly, it makes me feel connected in some small way to the women of my grandmother's generation who lived through the Depression, who had to think creatively about how to use their resources – turning old shirts into quilts and so forth. I think we consume far too much 'new' these days and I'd like to think I'm keeping certain skills of thriftiness alive, useful skills that I might be able to pass onto my daughter.

It's the fourth point, however – craft as a kind of therapy – that is most interesting to me, and definitely

Below: A stuffed menagerie.

Opposite, Top: Patchwork is a long-lasting trend.

Opposite, Bottom: Fiona's daughter models a custom-made skirt.

the most poignant. During difficult times in my life, I have often turned to craft. Craft has enormous distracting qualities. As good as a gripping novel, a good project can transport me somewhere else, turn my focus elsewhere. Plus, at the end, you have something for your efforts, something tangible and concrete. After the birth of my daughter, I battled for a year with post-natal depression. I found that burying my head in a craft project was just the kind of escapism I needed from the challenges of day-to-day baby-care. During this time I learned to knit again, and while my knitted creations from that time will never win awards, the process of making something, rediscovering a new skill just for myself, made me feel good. In no small part, it helped me through that difficult time.

inspiration

Aside from the usual suspects like colour, pattern, fabric, magazines and the internet, I find lots of inspiration in vintage clothes, textiles and crockery. I've had a life long 'thing' for the structured, heavy wool jackets and suits of the 1960s, knit vests and beautifully patterned women's dresses from the 1930s and '40s. I love things with a story, something that has been somewhere else before it came to you.

Something you can transform and hopefully breathe new life into, give a new use.

Without sounding too sentimental, however, these days my daughter is one of the biggest inspirations to me. There are so many fun things you can make for babies and young children: bibs, shoes, clothing, and toys. Also, I love seeing what patterns, colours and textures she is drawn to. The toys I now sell started as gifts for my daughter. I wanted to find some fun, slightly different soft toys for her, and when I couldn't find anything to my liking in shops, I started experimenting with sewing my own. Having a child has opened up a whole new world of crafting possibilities for me, for which I am immensely grateful. The colourful, friendly nature of children's clothing, toys and illustrated books inspires me every day.

workspace

Presently, my workspace consists a large old wooden table. It sits in the corner of an open thoroughfare in our home, adjacent to the main living area. For this reason, I try to keep it uncluttered, but it rarely is. On the table are my computer, sewing machine, and all manner of clear plastic and paper-covered boxes crammed full of thread, buttons, embellishments, paper and office supplies and lots of my favourite fat quarters. I like to keep them close to me! On the wall in front of me is my 'inspiration board' – a pin board overflowing with pictures that inspire, postcards, tear sheets from magazines, photos and fabric swatches. Here there are also shelves housing my craft books. Elsewhere in the room is an arts & crafts era hutch. This used to house our best china, but I have co-opted it for fabric storage. Under my table are large plastic tubs containing more fabric. Fabric storage is always a problem!

Above: Fiona's work desk.

Below: Fabric often ends up squeezed into every little space.

Opposite: A button for every project.

Library Tote

Directions on Page 136

about the project

This library tote is a favourite pattern. With a small child, I found we were visiting our local library more than ever before and using the same canvas bags we use to haul our fruit and vegetables from the market was just not cutting it!

This tote bag is quick and easy to make and can be embellished as little or as much as you desire. It has a simple but pretty pocket, which is big enough to hold a library card and a few other necessities. This tote can also be made to any shape or size that you like – to hold oversized picture books for children or novels and magazines for you.

Heidi Kenney

Location: Pennsylvania, USA   Occupation: Artist   Age: 28

Areas of Interest: Soft Toys   Website: http://www.mypapercrane.com/

why i create

When I was a child, my parents were always working on one project or another. From as far back as I can remember, my mother sewed. She had jobs creating elaborate window treatments, and then another creating tiny stuffed felt creatures at Annalee's doll factory. My father used to create landscape paintings that amazed me, and he sculpted little men out of clay. I have many early memories of my dad recording Bob Ross show's and then using them to teach himself to paint. I was always fascinated with his process, the big jar of brushes and tubes of oil paints.

My parents always encouraged me to explore my interest in creating. They bought art supplies for holidays, and we had free use over my mom's sewing machine since she first taught us to sew. At one point while I was growing up, my parents formed their own craft business, Jan-Jer Crafts, and I attended some craft shows with them. It seemed so surreal to me; they had business cards and could actually make money selling things they loved to make.

My two sisters and I would spend hours going through my mother's fabric scraps. We spent a whole summer once entertaining ourselves by making outfits out of the scraps (no sewing involved though, just draping). We would each take turns picking out just the right fabrics, and then arranging

them just so. We would also dress up our dolls in a similar fashion. Besides this interest in textiles, my sisters and I would experiment in the kitchen. For a big part of our childhood, we were latch key kids. So whenever we got home we would take out the cookbooks and look for new things to make. Most of the time it was cookies, or cakes, but we liked to make dinner dishes as well.

My older sister and I were very close in age, and once she came home with a present of handmade paper dolls she had made me. I loved them so much, but we were more interested in making them, instead of playing with them. We would spend hours creating new characters, the boys usually had black eyes (to show how tough they were), and the girls would have dresses with elaborate petticoats. We made up names for each of them; Taffy was one name we used too many times. We kept them all in a brown paper bag until the collection got too big, then it was transferred to a shoe box for safe keeping.

My mom taught all three of us to sew at a pretty young age. Our first projects were things like small doll items (blankets, pillows, etc.) And as we got older things like hair scrunchies. Though I really enjoyed sewing then, I did look at it as sort of a country habit. Something that wasn't very cool, and focused on country style crafts: things like sewing quilts and household decorations.

As I grew older, my focus turned more to painting and drawing. I think a lot of it had to do with my thoughts on sewing, plus once I moved out I didn't have a machine of my own. I drifted back to fabrics again anyway, taking up handsewing for quite some time. I worked on quilts for awhile, but could never really get excited about those projects. Then I started creating some little plush toys; in my mind they were for kids. I also worked on play food, all out of felt, and every piece sewn by hand. This was actually the first thing I sold online, but it would be a few more years before I made a business out of it.

My parents encouraged me to explore my interest in creating.

Opposite: Paper and fabric collage pieces.

Below: Boxes of Heidi's inspired creations.

I didn't get back into sewing with a vengeance until a few years later. I started again for fun with my own machine. Sometime while struggling again with what I thought you had to sew, I found a style of my own. I realized that sure, sewing machines can be used to make traditional items, but I could also create things of my own design with it as well. It sort of happened by accident. I was creating odd purses back then. Purses shaped like hedgehogs and ones that were sewn out of deconstructed stuffed animals. I had some scraps I was trying to use up (because I could never resist buying strange fabrics), and I found a long thin piece of brown vinyl-like fabric. I used the wrong side of the fabric as the crust for a slice of toast...and then things went on from there! While I liked making handbags, my actual love wasn't in the actual purse construction, but trying to make something odd into a purse. This is also how I started making purses shaped like toasters.

While most of my work time is used for sewing these days, I do like to experiment with all sorts of crafting. I spin yarn, I create with paper, and I still paint. Making things is something that just feels essential to everyday living to me. I find joy in creating anything with my hands...whether it be baking a cake or sewing an elaborate stuffed beast out of felt. I cannot imagine a time in my life where I won't be experimenting and making new things, I really feel it is just part of who I am.

inspiration

Everything I come in contact with motivates me to create, from large things like visiting art museums and seeing other people's artwork, to small things like peeling paint on a window ledge. I am inspired by the colors and textures of fabric. Sometimes just the right weave or print can inspire a whole new plush creation. My kids are also a huge source of inspiration for me. They like to give me ideas and challenges. My oldest son once told me he didn't think I could sew a glass of milk; that challenge was all I needed for inspiration, and sew one I did!

My husband is a tattoo artist and always inspires me with the things he is able to do on skin. Though he and I have totally different styles and mediums, his colors and artwork always inspire me. He is a great reminder that while making art might be a job, it is also something we do because we love it. I try to keep paper snips in a box, things that I like the color of, or maybe a pattern or typeset. I like going back through all the scraps. And while they may not contribute directly to a project, I think looking at the objects in our everyday life can be inspiring. Instead of looking out the window and seeing just the backyard, look closer, examine the way the leaves curl and the colors in the grass.

workspace

My studio is a room in my home. I have a long blue table that my husband built for me out of countertop. I use this area for sewing and sometimes even for paper projects. I have shelves for my fabric stash, but also keep shelves up in the attic to house it all. I have one table I set aside as a "packing" table. One reason I really like having my studio space in my home is that I feel I can work whenever the mood strikes. Many times I have gotten up out of bed at 2am because a brilliant idea has formed and I want to work on it right away.

I find joy in creating anything with my hands.

Opposite, Top: A crowd of cupcakes.

Opposite, Bottom: Heidi's studio storage.

Below: A beautiful old sewing machine, ready to work.

Tissue Cover

Directions on Page 138

about the project

I love houses. There is something about the idea of home that really stirs up good feelings inside me.

This is why I decided to create a house for my project – I love everything about a house. Whether it be the actual house itself, wall papers, shingles, and so on, or the idea of home being the place we retreat to. There is no place like home!

Hillary Lang

Location: Oak Park, Illinois   **Occupation:** Stay-at-Home Mom   **Age:** 36

Areas of Interest: Soft Toys, Quilting, Aprons, Bags, Pincushions   **Website:** http://www.weewonderfuls.com/

why i create

While I'm a sucker for the unique appeal of a handcrafted item, it truly is the process of crafting that keeps me hooked. Brainstorming new ideas is what I love, and the thrill of an idea coming together drives me to the sewing machine again and again. I swear there is an audible click when it all comes together in my head. That moment is the high I craft for.

Of course I'm not only an "idea gal." I definitely want to see projects through to conclusion, but I'm not one to relax and revel in my accomplishments. My head is always two or three projects ahead of my fingers. If I have one project in the sewing machine, I have at least two others cut out, fabric piled up for a couple more, and even more sketched out and ready to go. I don't try to fill up my workspace like this; but it's unavoidable. When a new idea pops into my head, it is all I can do to not immediately abandon my current project. I'll leave a project in the machine and go yank fabric for the new project, but that's as far as I'll let myself go. A little self discipline, the instinctual stopping point that keeps my mind from getting too far ahead of itself and the wonderful feeling of having a finished object all work together to keep me in check.

I often feel like I'm the sole contestant on a crafting reality show in my head. I set up challenges that I then must solve using the materials and knowledge

at my disposal—challenges such as making the cutest stuffed kitty doll, or the perfect not-too-big/not-too-small handbag, or coming up with the most beautiful way to reuse a thrifted floral sheet. To me, a wonderfully crafted item is like a puzzle, and I love solving puzzles. It's similar to other roles I've had in life, like debugging code or hunting down a fact for a patron at the library. I often trip over the solution. There always seems to be one key idea that clicks in place and makes the whole idea gel. Sometimes it's the very first idea, the spark. Sometimes it's the smallest detail that will finally make an idea come together, like the baby quilt I recently made for a friend. My big idea was to base the quilt on Grant Wood's beautiful landscapes, and I was trying to find the right mix of modern and quaint. I had stylized trees, a rolling hill line and a neat idea for really textural quilting, but it finally all came together when I picked out a great vintage tablecloth for the binding. The whole scene is surrounded by a blue sky binding and I'm finally satisfied with it. Of course, as soon as I cut the binding out I started yanking fabrics for a new stuffed toy idea.

The sense of satisfaction that comes from solving the riddle of a new project is even greater when the source of inspiration is something unexpected. Pouring through my stack of craft and design books and magazines can be limiting. I've stumbled upon some of my favorite designs when I wasn't even looking. The proportion in a great photograph triggers an apron design. The shape of an antique toy starts me on a toys on wheels kick. The jumper a friend made for her toddler gets reworked as a uniform for an army of big footed bunnies. On the other side, there was the quilt fiasco where I tried to make a clever patchwork from thrifted red shirts and ended up with a complete mess. I've had as many failures as successes when brainstorming "outside the box." When I'm working a project I often think of that scene in Pretty in Pink when Molly Ringwald is designing her prom dress from the two cast-off dresses, and she holds up a piece of ruffled sleeve to her forehead and then shakes her head at how

The smallest detail will make an idea come together.

Opposite: Vintage style animals on wheels.

Below: A trio of stuffed bunny toys

silly an idea it was. While the reconstructed dress she comes up with is notoriously bad, bravo for the process! Often the only way to get to a truly cool idea is through a lot of those head shaking moments.

The further away from my comfort zone I travel the more satisfying it is to actually complete a project. I love trying new things, learning new methods, investigating new mediums. I tend to jump into whatever new idea I have without much study or thought. I feel the more you know about how something is supposed to be done, the less fun it is. The internet is great for me because it is so easy to find quick how-to's for every possible craft. I grab the shortest answer to a question I can find and run with it. I often make mistakes this way, but to me they're nowhere near as discouraging as being overwhelmed by the entirety of a discipline. Also it's a lot more fun if you never know the rules.

inspiration

I used to think my inspiration changed with the wind. I have volumes and volumes of clipping books from the past ten or so years jammed full of things I've cut from magazines. Now, older and wiser, I can see when I look back through them

the trends and similarities. They're rooted in the imagery of my childhood, the certain indelible impressions my childhood surroundings imprinted on my subconscious. I am obsessed with a specific yellow – a bright saturated mustard yellow. Every time I see it somewhere I think I'm discovering it for the first time – in a photograph of the Carl Larsson house in Sweden, a painted wall in my Elle Decoration magazine. It just dawned on me recently that is the yellow of the painted wooden furniture in my childhood room. Now I see these childhood influences on my aesthetics so clearly – the illustrations in the books I read, the programs I watched on tv, the whole color palette of the 70s. Some things are more obvious than others, such as the love of modern Danish furniture that I inherited from my parents. Others are more deeply embedded and pop up when I'm least expecting them: Holly Hobbie, the folk art wallpaper pattern from my grandparents home, the simple wooden shaker boxes that all the women in my family treasure, the stylish glamour of my Magic Mary paper dolls, the dusty peachy pink that my grandmother loved, Lois Lenski and all the 40s and 50s illustration from my mother's childhood books.

I pick out all the fodder of Oscar's childhood with this in mind. While I have relaxed some about picking toys he'll actually play with over beautifully designed wooden toys with their timeless beauty, I still stop and consider every item I bring into our home. I look around our place and think about which things are creating those deep grooves in Oscar's psyche. I can't even pick out a coloring book for him without thinking of how he'll remember it twenty years from now.

A huge influence on my current crafting, besides my own childhood, is everyone's collective childhood. I'm obsessed with all things vintage and kid: toys, textiles, games, books, etc. I get so much inspiration from children's book illustration. The colors are amazing, the lines, the techniques they used, the fashions, the storytelling. I'm always picking up vintage kids clothes at the thrift store—whether they'll fit Oscar or not—the prints are so much fun. I especially love 70s message knits by Health-Tex. My favorite newborn outfit of Oscar's was a vintage onesie that had "I Heart Mommy. I Heart Daddy" printed all over it. I have an absurdly large collection of vintage kids books that I go back to time and time again for inspiration.

Opposite, Above: Shelves of craft and inspiration.

Opposite, Bottom: The ubiquitous inspiration board, covered with project ideas.

workspace

A workspace dedicated to crafting is the key to me getting anything done. I share a small home with a husband and a toddler, and carving out a little space for myself where I can lay everything out and have it still be in the same state when I return is a complete necessity. I want my entire home to be organized, but time and energy always seem to run out. The one place that I have to be organized is my craft room. It's a tiny room so everything needs to be in its place. Tucking things away and tidying up my workspace is one of my favorite relaxing activities. I've recently redone my room organization and now I'm happy as a clam in there.

My new button storage system: I used to have all my buttons in a printer's drawer, which was great for seeing them all at once but took up so much space. This new system of having them in small clear jelly jars nailed to the bottom of a shelf is such a space saver, looks very cool, and it is so satisfying to dump

Below: The ingenious button storage system.

out a tiny collection of buttons in my hand and run through them looking for just the right one.

My fabric: I stack my fabric on bookshelves and the stacks must be nice and neat so I can spy everything that's in them. If they start to get lumpy and lopsided I have to refold. I spend a lot of time refolding.

My display shelves: I really love my display shelves. I love to reorganize them and stage little scenes. All the toys and knick-knacks in there keep me company while I work. It's where I display all the amazing work that I've been lucky enough to trade or buy from fellow toymakers/bloggers.

My inspiration boards: I like to keep my inspiration boards spare enough that I can see what I have going on there. I've finally separated out my two worlds, if you will. One is for thriftcraft and is all fashion and accessories, and the other is for wee wonderfuls and is illustration, doll and toy design.

Above: A basket of cuties.

Below: A quilt shop? No, it's only Hillary's fabric shelves.

Opposite: Henny the doll takes a break.

Pillowcase Apron

Directions on Page 140

about the project

I can't pass up a cute pillowcase at the thrift store. Their conveniently small size makes it easy to take home an armload of vintage prints. They come already sewn up with finished edges, easily transformable into anything you can dream up – a skirt, bag, pillow, and here an apron.

This extremely simple project allows for customizable pockets galore without any cutting, fussy pressing or seaming. Perfect for a craft apron, cooking apron, hanging out apron, whatever you need. A package of twill tape and a pillow case and you're all set! Careful, they are addictive. You may end up making one for every apron-worthy occasion.

Juju Vail

Location: London, England   Occupation: Mother, Writer, Teacher   Age: Nearly 40

Areas of Interest: Clothing, Beading, Knitting, Painting   Website: http://jujulovespolkadots.typepad.com/

why i create

As long as I can remember I have had a crafting compulsion. My mind is obsessively preoccupied with designing and making things, all kinds of things.

Like many people with obsessions, I try to mask my extreme interest. I don't usually talk about it, but I'm thinking about it all the time. That look of polite interest on my face as I talk to you is really me working out how the collar of your shirt is constructed and enjoying the colour combinations in the poster on the bus behind you.

When I was eight, I was fascinated by a silver cat suit that one of Charlie's Angels wore when she was disguised as an alien (don't you just love those 70s plotlines). I wanted to make it so badly, but I didn't know anyone who could teach me to sew.

Family lore recounted my mother darning my father's socks with electric tape. There could be no help from that quarter.

So I taught myself.

From scraps of advice, library books and early experiments, I learned how to crochet, knit and sew before I was sixteen. I probably didn't do any of these with great skill, but I made up for it with enthusiasm. I seem to be blessed with the ability to

read and easily understand instructions. I have since learned that not everyone has this superpower. (My kryptonite would be spelling and mental maths. You can't have everything.)

I got a job in a fabric store and made clothes for myself and friends throughout high school. This was the early 80s when punk and new wave styles allowed a lot of dress freedom.

I took knitting with me everywhere. I even managed to do it secretly, under my desk, in school.

When I think back to these days I remember looking at textiles and clothes all the time. I went to quilt exhibitions, antique shops, fabric stores, always by myself, because I didn't know anyone my age who shared my intense interest. Luckily, I did have a couple of mentors in my late teens and early twenties. One was Anne Roberts, the artist mother of a boyfriend, another was Jone Baker, a knitwear designer I worked for. Their examples as women who lived and worked as artist/designers and mothers were important to me. They gave me a template of how my life could be. They were also very generous and taught me a lot.

I thought fashion college would be an oasis for me: a place where I could finally meet like-minded people and learn the skills I was dying to know. In some ways it was interesting; I loved and excelled in costume history, but I didn't find like-minded students. The others were more interested in fashion than clothes. They liked the constant changes and followed the styles in magazines.

My mind is preoccupied with designing and making things.

Opposite: A handmade shirt modelled by a mannequin designed by illustrator Maria Kalman – a junk yard find!

Below: Juju's work in progress.

I was interested in the hand-made and in textiles. I hated the way fashion glorified an idealized body and had nothing to say to anyone of a different shape, except maybe, "hide in black." I hated the fickleness and the waste of it.

I liked labour intensive embellishments that had no place in the Canadian garment industry I was training for. I had no interest in jeans, 'casual sportswear,' eveningwear or any of the usual industry categories. If there was a name for what I liked it might have been "costume for everyday wear." But who would wear this everyday costume?

I would. I dress in a creative, fun, some might say ridiculous, way. Everyday I enjoy putting my clothes together. I never wear jeans and I don't own a piece of black clothing (okay, except for underwear). I briefly tried a more conservative approach after the birth of my first child but it didn't last long and can be blamed on maternal madness. Now I get more outlandish with my clothing choices each year. I want to look like everyday is a celebration even if I'm just cleaning out my kitchen.

In my final years at fashion college I specialized in knitwear and millinery, which provided opportunities to design both the textile and garment shapes. This suited me better.

I left college early and set up a business designing hand and machine knitwear, which I had made by home workers. This did well but after a few years, my now husband and I decided to travel.

Later I came to London and did an MA in textile design. I continued to pursue an interest in hand-made items by specializing in hooked rugs. I studied, with fascination, the history of this craft and how antique rugs spoke of the people and places they came from. I made rugs entirely from recycled materials including old clothes and plastic bags, using personal imagery from my sketchbooks.

Since then, I have combined making things for exhibition and sale with writing about them in craft books and teaching.

Like a lot of blog authors, I have a family and a home to care for as well as my crafting work. I'm short on time and get easily bored and frustrated when I'm trying to produce volume for sale.

inspiration

Books are my greatest source of inspiration and information. I love the Internet for making the world my market place and connecting me to others with similar interests, but I still appreciate the experience of looking at books.

Antique ethnographic textiles and ornamentation really excite me. The idea that an Afghani girl will wear the embroidered bib of her childhood dress, reapplied to different garments, throughout her entire life, fascinates me! It interests me because of the value placed in the hand-made and the relationship between the clothing and the wearer. The embroidery is imbued with symbolism and meaning that endures. And the life of the textile, in the form of different garments, endures and acquires new value from its long association with the individual.

I also find these antique textiles immensely beautiful. I spend time drawing from books and in museums as I find it helps me to observe more closely.

I'm not trying to make work that looks like the ethnographic items I admire. I just try to let them make an impression on me and see how that filters through in my work.

I have recently taken up belly dancing and am really enjoying making my costume, which derives specific influence from the textiles and garment shapes of the Middle East and Asia. There is a vibrant community of American Tribal Style (also known as ATS) belly

My husband says I have a whim of iron; I constantly have new obsessions. As well as the crafts I have mentioned, I have experimented with jewelry, beading, polymer clay, glass bead making, felting, doll making, painting, printing, book making and other crafts.

Each new interest means collecting more tools and materials and learning new skills. A process I enjoy, but one that encumbers mastering a craft and requires lots of space and time.

I have long admired textile artists like Janet Bolton and Julie Arkell who have a single, steady vision and purpose in their work, but I'm afraid that, thus far, I'm not one of them.

However, at nearly forty, I'm beginning to see common threads in my interests and find ways to tie them together. Embellished textiles, dress, colour and pattern are common themes whether I'm painting, making sweaters or beading.

One of the reasons I began to blog about my crafts was to help me to focus and complete works. I didn't want my blog to be a self-indulgent diary but I did want to be more conscious of why I was doing what I was doing and how one interest led to and influenced another.

Opposite, Top: A beaded cuff.

Opposite, Bottom: Detail from one of Juju's unique skirts.

Above: A whimsical collage.

dancers who make their own costumes influenced by the nomadic tribal people of these areas. Their Internet community shares advice and style ideas in much the same way the craft blogging community does.

Colour is a very important feature of all my work and I'm never far from my paints. In the last few years I've been taking my painting more seriously. Where previously it was a means to record and develop ideas, I now spend more time painting for its own sake. I like to paint ideas of the things that inspire me but make them work as pictures in their own right.

Many painters have influenced me, including colourists like Bonnard, and Matisse, as well as more contemporary painters. I love the watercolour still-lifes of Jenny Wheatley and the landscapes of Scottish painter Barbara Rae..

I love the way that watercolour paintings display the entire process of painting. Nothing is concealed. All mistakes and experiments are on display.

I think embracing accidents is a very important and exciting part of the creative processes; one that needs to be harnessed in art and craftwork in order to prevent it from looking too dull and masterly.

work space

I work from a North-facing studio in my London home, where I sometimes teach small classes. Several years ago I spent £400 on great halogen lighting. It really makes working in the dark English winters and evenings much easier. However, I still find winter photography a problem and am now saving for some photographic lighting.

It is the largest room in our house but still doesn't feel nearly big enough as it holds a plan chest, small sofa, computer, printer, desk, folding easels, painting trolley, chairs, ironing board, filing cabinet, sewing machine, jewelry work bench, cutting and sewing tables, and storage furniture. In stacked tins and labeled boxes I house my collection of paints, fabrics, beads, buttons, ribbons, yarn, fleece, art materials, tools, papers, ephemera, CDs, books and more books. That sounds terribly cluttered but I do put away and take out things depending on what I'm working on. My beading table and computer desk are always set up and ready to go. There is little wall space but a pin board and washing line hold inspiring images and items. I love being in here.

Opposite, Top: Cats love crafts.

Opposite, Bottom: Pieces of a collection.

Above: Stylish vintage tins.

Pebble Bracelet

Directions on Page 142

about the project

I play around with felt, beads and silk a lot. I love the way each of these materials captures brilliant colours in very different textures and I love to mix them together.

In this bracelet I have felted 'pebble' beads with silk scrap inclusions. I chose a neutral colour for the felt so that the silk scraps would really pop. But of course the colours, sizes and textures beg to be experimented with.

It sort of looks like something Pebbles Flintstone might wear. Great for the winter, when a delicate bracelet would get overwhelmed my sweaters.

Katey Nicosia

Location: Dallas, Texas   **Occupation:** Designer, Craft Entrepreneur   **Age:** 25

Areas of Interest: Totes, Purses, Pin Cushions, Soft Toys   **Website:** http://www.onegoodbumblebee.com/

why i create

I remember being four-years-old, waking up one morning to a toasted bagel and my father setting up a blank t-shirt and several bottles of fabric paint on the kitchen table for my sister and I. He told me to do whatever I wanted to the shirt, to write my name on it, perhaps. To decorate it. I don't know why he chose this particular activity on that particular morning, but I remember thinking that it was a wonderful way to start the day. And it didn't matter that I ended up decorating the back of the t-shirt instead of the front because I was four, and at four years old rules like "the tag goes in the back" don't really mean anything. All I knew was that I created something, and in my little world of paint and blank t-shirt, no rules existed.

I've always known that I'm lucky to have creative parents, parents that kept buckets of markers and crayons in the kitchen cabinets, who put me in art classes, taught me how to draw a three-dimensional box, and ultimately encouraged me to be someone who makes things. Surprisingly, though, I grew up dreaming of becoming an elementary school teacher, but it wasn't until college, where I majored in Education and experienced teaching first hand, that I realized that being a teacher was never what I really wanted. Instead, what attracted me to teaching were the materials involved. The papers, pens, stickers, a decorated room, construction paper and glue. And much to everyone's surprise, I

switched gears away from the teaching profession and began to pursue what I'd actually wanted all along: to be an artist.

I didn't have a plan or real idea of what I wanted to create but I knew that I wanted to own my own shop and sell my creations. Without hesitation, I called my father and told him about my new pursuit. I remember saying bluntly, "I want to start a business," and then giggling to myself because at the time it sounded crazy and over ambitious, but I didn't care. I went full-force at the beginning and started One Good Bumblebee without any clue as to how to own and manage a business. And honestly, at that time, the "business" side wasn't important. I wasn't formal about taxes, income, or receipts because all I wanted was to make things that people could buy and use. So I designed the One Good Bumblebee website, whipped up a few purses and pouches and added them to the site. And before I knew it, people bought them, and I started to get requests and demands for more. It wasn't until about a year or so later that I started to think not only like an artist but like a business owner. I have to take into account my customers and their needs and wants, the price of materials, packaging, how I might photograph the item for the website, and so much more. It can be difficult to separate the "thinking" from the whim of creating an art piece, and it's something I still

struggle with today. It always helps, though, to tell myself to play, to remind myself that for me, being an artist comes before being a business owner, to relax and to always have fun.

Today, I still run One Good Bumblebee by myself and all my products are still designed and created by me. At times, running a one-woman craft business can be very overwhelming and demanding but it's always rewarding and exciting. I know with One Good Bumblebee that I've found my niche, the perfect job for me.

Being an artist comes before being a business owner.

Opposite: Four-year-old Katey decorates her t-shirt.

Below: Inspiring trinkets on a line.

inspiration

Nothing motivates or inspires me more than a new stash of fresh fabric, a perfectly sharpened pencil, or a new set of watercolors. There are so many possibilities instilled in something unused, that I often can't help discovering what one of those possibilities might be. It's an urge, a pull, an instinct that never fails. If I ever find that I've lost motivation or that I can't think of anything to make, a trip to an art supply store is usually the best cure.

I get a lot of my ideas from my childhood, or from what used to be. I'm inspired by the past or anything old, anything with a story behind it, like antique binoculars or the pattern on a pair of vintage pillow cases. One of my favorite sources of "old" is Ebay. I could spend hours upon hours looking at the items up for auction, drinking in their shapes, colors and uses. I almost always come away with a new idea, a new spark to start my next project.

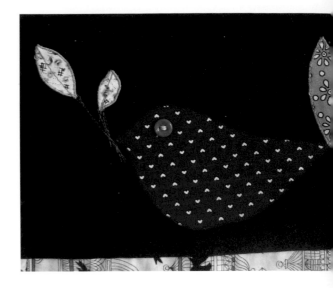

Another major source of inspiration for me is other artists. Sometimes it helps to look at what other artists are making to get my own gears in motion. There's something special about looking at a fellow artist's creation and walking away with an idea of my own. I feel there's a relationship between artists in that way, and I love to look at something brilliant made by a favorite artist that intrigues me and in turn encourages me to be just as brilliant.

workspace

My workspace is small, intimate and often chaotic. In one part of the room, you could find a pile of paper scraps and in another, a box of vintage buttons or a tangle of colorful ribbons. I have a section for packaging my products, one for cutting papers, another for sewing projects, and others for every craft project imaginable.

My ideal workspace would be gigantic, an open room with a long table in the middle for cutting fabrics and paper. The walls would be lined with shelves stacked with perfectly labeled boxes, and pretty jars of buttons and knick-knacks. Oh what a dream! But of course a room like that is far from possible for me right now, and so I make the most of my tiny room, and I mean that almost literally.

Sometimes I like to get out of my little room and work in other parts of my house. It helps me "get out" and work in a new atmosphere, even if I'm just one room away. A lot of times, I pack up my materials and plop in front of the TV in the den and work there. Other times I spread out on the floor in the living room and work on my hands and knees like I did as a kid. It's always fun and sometimes necessary to make a mess, to spread out and see what's before me, to see what I have to work with.

I must admit that my craft room is rarely neat and tidy and is almost always in disarray. At times the chaos can be daunting and hectic, and it's never easy to find my best scissors or that perfect black pen. But the disorder isn't necessarily a bad thing, but reflects the fact that I've been working, that I'm in the middle of a project, or that I've recently had a brilliant idea and I'm trying to bring it to life. I like to think of my cluttered studio as a good thing, as a reminder that I'm an artist and there's nothing else I'd rather be.

Opposite, Top: An applique design for a purse.

Opposite, Bottom: A unique button cuff.

Below: Fun toys mixed with professional products on Katey's desk.

Ice Cream Pin Cushion

Directions on Page 141

about the project

This is one of my favorite projects because it's super easy, quick, useful and lends itself to endless creative designs. Pin cushions, in general, are so much fun to make because you can use almost any object as its base, add a little padding and fabric and voila! But there's something special about a tiny pin cushion meant to hold only a few special pins, because it's not only functional but also charming and can really add a little fun to sewing!

This pattern has endless variations: use red and white polka dot fabric and make a mushroom or use skin-colored fabric and embroider a face to make people pin cushions. The opportunities are endless, so you should definitely be creative and have fun with this project. The pattern is so simple and quick, you might find yourself addicted to making them, but don't fret; they make great gifts for all your crafty friends!

Lisa Congdon

Location: San Francisco, California   **Occupation:** Education Consultant   **Age:** 38

Areas of Interest: Ephemera, Sewing, Painting, Collages   **Website:** http://birdinthehand.typepad.com/

why i create

For me, all of my creative endeavors are intensely intimate and spiritual. I suffered from chronic depression and anxiety in my late twenties and early thirties. It was at age thirty-three that I decided I was tired of feeling so horrible all of the time, and that I ought to get to know myself better, to face whatever I was afraid of, and to find what made me happy.

I was fortunate enough to find an amazing therapist, who happened also to be an amazing teacher, and who helped me to see that I was so much more than my physical body; that I was, indeed, a spiritual being with incredible creative potential. This was the great turning point in my life. I went off anti-depressant medication and delved into looking at everything about myself—what I feared, what had shaped who I was, and what I was passionate about. When I got stuck, I worked it out by writing or painting or drawing.

It was during this time that my creative life took off. I had always made stuff, and I always loved art and design. I grew up in a family of crafters and artists and was always surrounded by artistic mediums and opportunities to invent something new. But this time it was different. I realized then that I *had* to make things; it was no longer just a hobby. It became my new anti-depressant.

At first, everything I made or drew or painted was for me. I didn't even tell people that I was spending my alone time working at my kitchen table. At the time, I lived in a very small studio apartment. And then, bit-by-bit, I started to reveal my creations to others. I painted and sewed, and I kept journals filled with writing and painting and photographs. I shared them with trusted souls, family members and close friends and lovers. And for a time, this is what fed me.

And then there is something truly amazing that happens when you discover you not only love to do something, but that you are quite good at it. And it happens when a wide-array of outsiders (not just your lover or mother) lets you know that your work is pleasing to their senses.

This is what happened to me. And it was a most life-affirming discovery. I think we all live to express our true selves, to live up to something or to be something or somebody. We want to be understood, to connect with others and to be loved even when we reveal the darkest or most vulnerable sides of ourselves. And through my artwork and crafts, I felt a deep connection with myself and others that I had never felt before.

It was then that I ventured out into the cyberspace and began my own blog through which I shared my creations and thoughts about everyday life. And what started slowly and tentatively has become one of the greatest joys of my life. Through my blog, I have had the opportunity to connect with other creative souls around the planet. And in this community of crafters and artists, we share our work, critique, affirm, adore, and befriend. No longer is my immediate circle of friends and lovers and family my inspiration and audience. Now I have the world.

And so I am motivated everyday to make something new: take a new photograph; try a new pillow design; share a new collage; create a new drawing — and then to share it with a thousand other people. This has kept me more alive than I have ever been.

I am motivated every day to make something new.

Opposite: Stencils on Lisa's inspiration board.

Below: One of Lisa's trademark log-cabin cushions.

And now when I do feel depressed or anxious — because I am human and sometimes I still feel those things — I can create something new, and it grounds me entirely. Or I can go read another crafter's blog and feel inspired by what they have made. It's a really wonderful daily experience.

inspiration

My mind is always filled with ideas. In fact, I have a number of small notebooks in my bag and lying around my office and apartment on which I have scribbled sketches or notes or lists of ideas. I am famous at work for losing concentration in long meetings, because I am drawing something or making long schematic maps of interweaving ideas. My coworkers tolerate it, because generally I am well organized and a good thinker and contributor to the work, and I do think they value the creative energy I bring to our somewhat cerebral daily tasks.

So I am never at a loss for what to make. I just don't have the time or money for supplies or the technical skill to execute all of my ideas. I make do with the time and supplies and technical skill that I do have. And I generally dive right into projects. My mother used to tease me when I was a kid because whenever

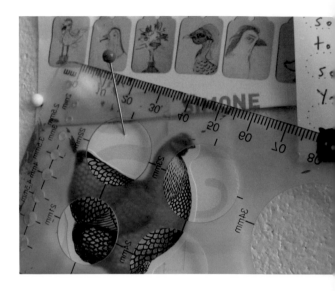

I decided that my bedroom should look different or that I needed a new look, I would simply go for it, without thinking it through—I could not wait for help or suggestions; in fact, I couldn't have cared less about help or suggestions.

And so it is generally the same today. I get inspired by a lot of things, all the time. I write the ideas down so I don't lose them, and then I begin making whatever I am feeling like. There is no charting or graphing. Rarely are there patterns. My sister and mother and I are all artists and crafters, and we are all like this. We work from our gut. We try and experiment. We use our intuition and figure it out. Later in this book I will describe how to make a unique log cabin pillow. I have never used a pattern for this or read directions. So writing them for others has been quite an interesting experience!

People often ask me where my ideas come from and what inspires me. That is a hard question for me

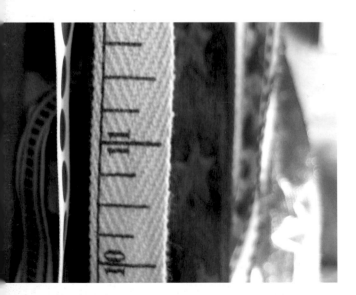

Above: Keeping inspiration and tools handy.

Left: Unique trims and ribbons make a project special.

Opposite: Margaret the Cat keeps an eye on things.

to answer, because I am a very visual person who notices every minute detail in very ordinary things. So it might be a crack in the wall or the way colors are painted on the side of a building. It's not unusual for me to take my camera around with me as I run errands in my neighborhood to capture colors and shapes and contrasts that inspire me. But the usual things also inspire me: nature (I love bird and tree and wood imagery), poetry, and certainly other people's art. I also love fashion and bold graphic design. Living in an urban area rich with different cultures and an abundance of art — both in the street and in galleries — makes for never-ending inspiration. The art scene in San Francisco is amazing, and I go to art shows here in San Francisco regularly.

I think I am most known for my love and use of color in all of my work. I am surrounded by it where I live in the Mission District. I love working with colorful vintage and contemporary fabrics and using muted bright color in my artwork. I wear colorful clothes (though I'm also known to wear all black from time to time). I have colorful walls in my apartment. I take color photography with a film that takes super saturated photographs.

In the end, in order to feel inspired, it's important to have a certain level of openness to the beauty and energy that is around you. And I think that's the most important thing. It's not so much what inspires you, but that you are inspired to create. In my experience, true inspiration is accompanied by a feeling of joy. When I am inspired, I am never so joyful. And some days I am so inspired that I can take bits and pieces of it and save them for days when I am feeling depressed or frightened.

workspace

One of the places in which I try to contain all of my inspiration is my studio. My friend Nathalie calls my apartment "organized chaos," because I have so many interesting things around, but they are all placed purposefully as if to make a statement. And I think my small studio epitomizes this characterization. It's so small, in fact, that I often have to spread projects to my bedroom (which is conveniently attached by a large opening) or to the kitchen or living room. When I bought this apartment, it was important to me that I have a room to make a studio after I moved from my small one-room apartment. And so while it doesn't have many of the amenities I hope to someday have — a utility sink with running water, really good lighting, ample shelf storage and a huge cutting table — it is still my studio, and it is my favorite room.

Two years ago one of my best friends built me a worktable and covered an entire wall with corkboard so I could pin every inspiration to it. This is one of my favorite features. My studio's not very big, so things are stuffed in every nook and cranny and it's generally very messy. I try to keep my fabric collection neat and organized and sorted by color,

otherwise it's really hard to find what I want when I start a project!

My cats like my studio too. They are known to bat all of my small supplies out of the many compartmentalized trays I collect and play with them all night long as I sleep. And they somehow like my sewing chair better than the bed or sofa. It's covered in their fur and I rarely vacuum it off. My studio is all about me. And when people come to visit, it's the room they like to visit most too, even though it doesn't have plates of food in it or a sofa or a television. They love to look around. And that gives me a wonderful feeling…and makes me feel, well, more inspired.

Below and Opposite: Keeping everything on hand for constant crafting.

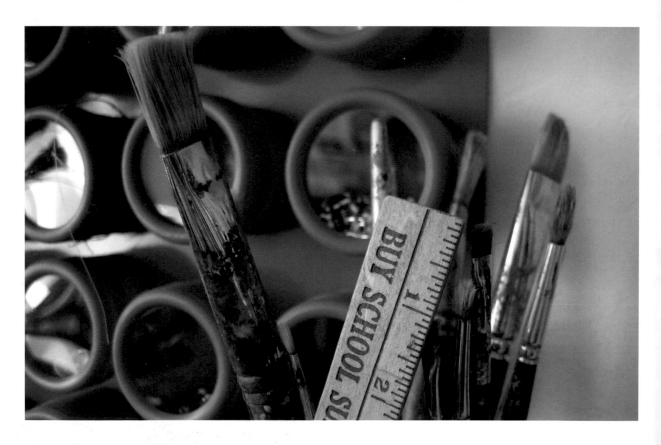

Log Cabin Pillow

Directions on Page 144

about the project

I first began making machine-made log cabin pillows when I acquired a wonderful Japanese craft book that featured them. I was drawn to them immediately and began creating my own using a mix of colorful vintage and contemporary fabrics.

That was nearly a year ago, and I haven't stopped making them since! Very traditional log cabin squares use only three different fabrics and contrast light to dark fabrics in opposing corners. I piece my log cabin pillows together using the traditional pattern, but they are a far cry from the traditional design. I play with a mixture of solid and patterned fabrics—sometimes up to 16 different fabrics in large pillows—bold colors, text, and patches. My favorite part of making each of my pillows is selecting the fabrics I will use. Piecing the fabrics together strip by strip to create a balanced, interesting and beautiful piece is an incredibly satisfying aesthetic experience.

Lyn Roberts

Location: Devon, England   **Occupation:** Stay at Home Mum   **Age:** 45

Areas of Interest: Soft toys, Scarves, Bags, Baby Quilts   **Website:** http://mollychicken.blogs.com/

why i create

I have always crafted; one of my earliest memories is sitting with my mother, watching her sew. We were always encouraged to try things ourselves; I still have a little teddy bear that we made together, when I was about five years old. I grew up surrounded by women who had large families and little money, so there were children's clothes to be made and mended, husbands' socks to darn, and scratchy woollen jumpers to knit.

My father knew how to knit and sew too, something he learned whilst serving in the British Navy during World War Two. Sailors were expected to be able to repair their uniforms while at sea and embroidered many pieces for their sweethearts at home to while away the time. Even though my father had huge hands, with fingers like big fat sausages, he could sew the tiniest, neatest stitches.

My mother refused to buy anything she thought she could make herself; this was something that caused me great embarrassment as a teenager – I wanted a school scarf like everybody else's, not a hand knitted effort.

Now though, it seems like I'm becoming more like my mother every day. I, too, now prefer to make rather than buy. I particularly enjoy recycling old fabrics; I love to trawl around my local charity/thrift shops looking for textiles. My soft toys are usually

made from old woollen blankets that are felted in a hot machine wash, and then dyed to produce a huge palette of colours.

Old curtains, velvet cushion covers, and children's clothing are other favourites of mine, all supplying a fabulous array of colours, prints, and textures.

Crafting is something that saves my sanity; it provides a very welcome escape from my busy, hectic life. Small children are invariably noisy, bless them, so to be able to sit in my craft room, sewing, listening to the sound of nothing is heavenly. I particularly enjoy embroidery, because it can be done in silence, although I do love my sewing machine with a tremendous passion.

Creating something unique from an assortment of odds and ends is very satisfying; giving a soft toy its own character by placing its features in a certain way is great fun. I've learnt that it's best not to get too "precious" when it comes to crafting. I find exactness stifling and no longer worry about features being symmetrical or whether one arm is higher than the other– in fact it all adds to the charm of a thing.

I am very grateful to my parents for bringing us up with a "You can do that" attitude, they believed that something should always be attempted, even if you mess up, so my one piece of advice would be: don't be afraid of that fabric – give it a go!

inspiration

Inspiration can come from anywhere: helping out at arts and crafts sessions at my children's school is always a good source. The children I work with are at an age where their "inner critic" hasn't kicked in yet, so they create with gay abandonment. The colours they put together and their pleasure in drawing something without worrying about perspective or accuracy is a joy to watch. Picasso once said that

Don't be afraid of that fabric – give it a go!

Opposite: Bundles of Lyn's hand-dyed wool

Below: A gorgeous pile of crafts.

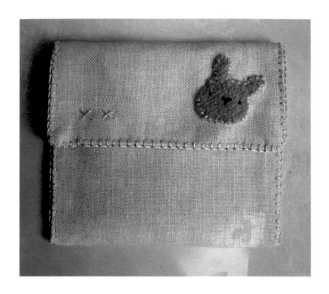

and Alan Ahlberg, Richard Scarry, Olwyn Whelan, Emma Carlow, Brian Wildsmith and many others.

Finally, the Internet – ah the wonderful Internet, what can I say that hasn't already been said? Far, far too much time is spent staring in awe at my computer screen.

workspace

I work from home, in what was originally the dining room of our Edwardian house. The room is north facing, which makes it perfect for storing my fabrics – no direct sunlight to fade them. I have French doors that allow a lot of light in, and which lead to a little courtyard where I like to sit and sew in the summer.

he spent a lifetime trying to unlearn everything that had been taught to him at art school, so that once again, he could paint from the heart like a child. So I usually come away from these sessions inspired by a little person Above all, they remind me that creating something is supposed to be fun- something that's easy to forget when you're stressing over your French seams .

Vintage fabrics are another inspiration for me. I love children's prints from the last century, particularly the 1950s, 60s, and 70s. I also have a collection of vintage dresses made by the Dutch children's label, Oilily. They excel at producing bold and beautiful items of clothing with colours and patterns that clash in the most wonderful way. Again, I suppose it's all about not paying any attention to any rigid rules when it comes to design.

Sticking with the childhood theme, children's illustration is something that I also find very inspiring. Having had four children, we have a vast supply of books at home, I particularly love the work of Janet

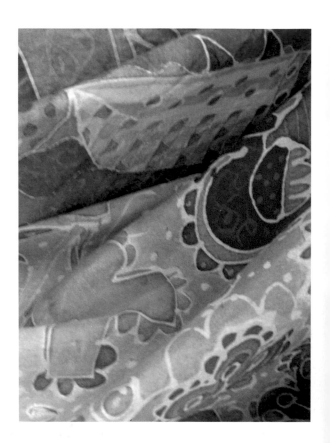

Above: A simple purse in Lyn's unique style.

Right: Beautiful hand painted silk.

There's a beautiful fireplace, whose mantelpiece holds soft toys made by fellow crafters, baskets of beads and sequins, my children's artwork, and some of my cherished books. There is also an old Chemist's cupboards bought at an auction, which houses some of my rather large fabric stash. I have a big old desk, which is my main work area, and three large units, which my very clever husband made, to store my books, bits, bobs, boxes, and yet more fabric.

Right: Lyn's fabric collection, including vintage Oilily patterns, give a special look to her projects.

Below: Animals on parade.

Children remind me that creating is supposed to be fun.

Patchwork Purse

Directions on Page 135

about the project

I designed this purse as a project to gently ease beginners into the wonderful world of sewing. It can be kept simple and completed in a couple of hours, or you can invest more time and embellish away to your heart's content.

This purse can be hand or machine stitched, and can be interlined with a commercial stiff interfacing for a sharp smart look, or interlined with 3 or 4 layers of a soft cotton fabric for a soft squashy look.

The detachable corsage is simplicity itself, just layers of petals held together by a few stitches and a button or bead. Feel free to add sequins or decorative embroidery stitches and whatever else takes your fancy.

Maitreya Dunham

Location: New Jersey, USA   Occupation: Scientist, Teacher   Age: 28

Areas of Interest: Embroidery, Sewing, Screen-Printing   Website: http://www.craftlog.org/

why i create

It all started one day when I was in elementary school, when my mother took me and my sisters to a store that sold cross stitch kits and let us each pick one out. I still have the project, a little bag with a goose on it. It was a slippery slope from there. I started searching for pattern books and collecting colors of thread, and my mom commissioned a set of placemats (one of which is still not done).

I did mainly cross stitch until I started picking up other things in college. I went to MIT, which has two normal semesters separated by a month long "independent activities period," during which anybody can teach short classes. I took a quilting class taught by one of my classmates one year, which was an entree into sewing and fabric crafts. After that I made a quilted pillow of the MIT great dome in florals, which at the time I thought was a great ironic object. It fell apart one day when I tried to wash it. I'm still sad it's gone.

One of my main inspirations for crafting soon became Martha Stewart's magazines and books. I started a little journal to keep track of which issues had the projects I wanted to try. That journal was the first incarnation of my crafting website, Craftlog. Both of my sisters had been keeping blogs for quite a while and were more plugged in to the online community than I was. One of my sisters made everybody marble magnets for Christmas one year, and told me she found the directions on a craft blog, Not Martha.

That's what introduced me to the whole online craft community. I started Craftlog a few months later, mainly as a way of procrastinating while writing my PhD thesis, but also as a way to share my work with the growing craft blog universe.

How that community has grown over the three years I've been blogging has just been mind-blowing. It's a large part of my continued experimentation with different crafts and a huge source of encouragement and ideas.

My family has also encouraged my craftiness. I fondly remember going with my grandma to garage sales one summer, picking up bags of trims, pompoms, felt, and whatever else I could glue together to make something. She was a crocheter, a craft I didn't pick up until years after she died, and just one of my crafty relatives. We always had quilts made by my great grandma or various great aunts, another craft I didn't pick up until much later. In fact, my first large quilt was made of blocks pieced by some unknown relative and found hidden in a closet. My sisters and I also always made stuff, from knotted embroidery thread bracelets to playhouses in the woods. One of my sisters is still an avid cross-stitcher, and my other sister is also very creative. My mom does stained glass and beading, and my sister-in-law taught me to knit. My niece just told me that crafting is one of her favorite things, so maybe it'll go even another generation.

None of this really answers the question of why I craft, though. Primarily, I just enjoy making things. I enjoy doing a bit of embroidery while I'm watching TV, or picking out the perfect fabric for a new bag. I like to make crafts that enhance my apartment, that I enjoy wearing, that I'm proud to give as gifts.

inspiration

What's funny to me is how many of the branch points in my crafting development are so cliched in many ways. Friendship bracelets? Cross-stitched geese, Martha Stewart, and marble magnets? Even the self-consciously ironic craft has become a cliche

The growth of the on-line community has been mind-blowing.

Opposite: The fateful goose that started it all.

Below: A drawer of goodies.

with all the "not your grandmother's crafting" type books and websites.

The internet has really opened up a much broader array of influences so I can move beyond these cliches into more creative territory. Craft bloggers are great about linking inspiring artists, designers, and shops which I might never have come across on my own. Not to mention all the wonderful things that everyone makes. I read about one hundred craft blogs so I am never at a loss for beautiful images and great ideas.

But I'm also still inspired by Martha Stewart. The level of quality and skill her magazines encourage has always been a plus to me rather than the much reviled "perfectionism" some people demean it as. For a long time, she was the only even vaguely modern mainstream crafting portal. Now there's more available in books, magazines, and on TV, so I don't rely on her as much.

I am always on the lookout for creative and modern craft books. My local library has a great craft books section, from which I almost always have an armful checked out. The public library is great this way because I can get books that I wouldn't use enough to justify buying, but that have maybe one

or two appealing projects. It's also a great way to investigate new crafts.

Japanese craft books in particular are my new favorite inspiration, though. The very clean, very modern aesthetic is appealing to me in a way I no longer feel for cross-stitched geese.

workspace

I am lucky enough to have a devoted craft room. My craft table is a computer desk, which I really like because the space under the desk where the computer is supposed to sit is just perfect for my sewing machine. One end of the table has a cutting mat, right next to a pegboard wall for my scissors, rotary cutter, jeweler's saw, and other tools. The cabinets and shelves around the room are pretty much a mess, with supplies stuffed everywhere. I like to go overboard with the supplies. I like craft supplies in and of themselves. Fabric and yarn and colored thread are just pretty. Having every color of

Gocco-printing ink or embroidery thread is also nice because when I feel like crafting something, I more than likely already have the materials.

I keep all my fabrics in two cabinets of little cubbies that I think must be meant for storing shoes. I like having the fabric easily accessible and all in sight so I can browse for what I need or even start with an appealing piece of fabric as inspiration for a project. I often start projects in this way, beginning with the materials and imagining what they could be. I am starting to get good enough at sewing and crochet that I can draft my own patterns for simple things, but mostly I use patterns from books or the internet.

I typically have several projects going at once, a couple of long-term ones interspersed with instant-gratification crafts. I also keep an idea list tacked to my cork board along with pretty cards, embroidery swatches, nice letters from my "imaginary friends" in blogland, and whatever else seems visually appealing. Whenever I'm at a loss for a project, I check the list and see if I feel like starting anything new. I have folders of inspiring magazine and catalog pages for browsing as well.

My computer is as much a crafting tool as my sewing machine. I run craftlog with Movable Type, and I try to update the site design every few months. Keeping all my links organized is also quite a challenge, but I have a system for sorting everything into folders for safe-keeping. Once a month or so, I go back through my bookmarks and decide what links should be posted on my website. I have learned the hard way to just download pictures and instructions for projects I might want to try. You never know when a favorite site might disappear.

Opposite, Top: A pretty, pleated bag.

Opposite, Bottom: A machine embroidered garden.

Below: Versatile fabric storage.

Desk Organizer

Directions on Page 146

about the project

These embroidered felt organizers really reflect on me as a crafter, my influences and what I value in a project. Once I got this thick felt on a trip to Japan, a steal at 350 yen, I knew it was destined to be a box of some variety. Add in a messy sewing desk drawer, and the project came together. It is both useful and pretty. I always enjoy making more craft tools (pin cushions, sewing machine cover, needle books, etc) that I can enjoy every time I create something else.

The illustration style of the sewing box embroidery seems like it belongs in a Japanese craft book, a fitting match for the felt. The hand embroidery on the sewing box, partnered with the candy color scheme, script labels, and vintage pillowcase fabric backing, is pretty and nostalgic. The felt box itself, unadorned, seems so geometric and simple, though, that it has a modern appeal as well. I've tried to emphasize those qualities in the desk tray variation. Although the felt box base is the same, matching it with machine-embroidered sketches in graphic black and white gives it a completely different feel.

The box does not have enough structural support to cart it around, which is why I have designed it as a desk organizer. It is surprisingly sturdy, though; a prototype has survived 4 months of use without incident. If you plan to store, say, pencils, in it, a darker color for the walls is recommended to hide any marks. The use of high quality felt is important since craft felt will pill quickly and is less dense. If you're lucky, you can find thick felt at a craft or fabric store. If not, "industrial felt," "press cushion," and "press blanket" are good keywords to try on the internet. You can also fuse together 2 or 3 layers of normal thickness felt or use felted knits.

Mariko Fujinaka

Location: Portland, Oregon   **Occupation:** Writer and Editor   **Age:** 40

Areas of Interest: Knitting and Sewing Clothes, Bags   **Website:** http://www.supereggplant.com/

why i create

Is it nature or nurture that brought me to crafting? I am of Japanese descent, and I have always found the Japanese to be prone to artistic and crafty endeavors, regardless of background or profession. A spirit of aesthetics permeates the culture; it is inescapable. I come from a long line of crafters, but none of them were consumed by craft – it was simply second nature.

My grandmother in Japan was always knitting or crocheting, and even when she began losing her sight to macular degeneration, she knit. I still have the ruby red, cabled cardigan sweater she knit for me, even though it hasn't fit for over a decade. When I think about my aunt in Japan, I envision her constantly creating. The first time I visited Japan, I was four. During that visit my aunt made dolls for my brother and me. My brother's doll was supposed to look like our father. He wore a striped sweater and sported a jaunty beret. My doll was, I think, supposed to represent my mother, but my aunt made the mistake of letting me select the hair color and the buttons for the eyes. Well, mine had orange hair and clear button eyes. I still have that doll (though she doesn't have much hair left). Through the years my aunt has continued to make various things – she knit me numerous sweaters, both by hand and with a knitting machine, crocheted dishrags, crafted classic Japanese dolls – you name it, she made it.

My mother has always claimed she is not particularly crafty. She feigns disinterest in sewing and knitting and crafting, but during my childhood, she was constantly creating amazing items. My mother sewed nearly every single one of my outfits until I hit fourth grade and decided to become a tomboy. I remember many of the dresses she made for me: for my second grade school picture I wore a long-sleeved orange dress with a white leaf pattern (It was a little scratchy. Polyester was dismayingly popular during my youth.); for the third grade photo I wore a dotted Swiss dress with poofy sleeves; in fourth grade, the last dress I allowed her to make for me was a multicolored polyester knit outfit, which I recall as being a tad clingy. At one point she got really into Frostline Kits; she sewed down booties for the whole family, rain parkas, backpacks, and down vests. My mother also knit like a fiend, embroidered, tatted, hooked rugs, and even made jewelry. She was truly a renaissance woman and one of my greatest influences.

Another person who significantly influenced me and gave me cause to craft is Mrs. H, the mother of Alice, a childhood friend. Alice and I became friends in first grade, and every time I went to her family's house, I would discover her mother ensconced in her sewing room, surrounded by piles and piles of fabric. There were three girls in the family, and they all wore beautiful handmade clothing. Not only did Mrs. H sew, but she also knit. She even opened two fabric stores, one specializing in all-natural fibers with luxurious silks and wools and linens. The daughters are adults now, two with children of their own, yet Mrs. H continues to feverishly sew and knit, making outfits for the children and the grandchildren and all their friends and neighbors!

Surrounded by this constant crafting, maybe it was inevitable that I would pick up the needles and break out the scissors. Alice and I enrolled in a summer sewing class when I was about nine. We had a tough time, but I still remember what I made:

I come from a long line of crafters – it was second nature.

Opposite: A SuperEggplant original.

Below: Mariko hard at work – in a vest she knit herself!

a short-sleeved orange terry cloth top, complete with hood. It didn't fit very well, but I still loved it. I also remember the first sweater I knit. I think I was about ten or eleven when I asked my mother to teach me how to knit. I made a crewneck sweater vest that buttoned up the back. It was made of very, very thick grey wool.

So I suppose this crafting thing is a compulsion. It got into my blood, and once I started, I could not stop. It didn't even matter that I was not particularly gifted (I won't confess how many times I've sewn pockets to the bottoms of trouser legs). I spent countless hours at Alice's house, sewing this or that with Mrs. H's patient guidance. My mother and I knit together and went to craft stores to dabble in the latest craft crazes. Crafting comes in waves – for a couple years I will become so obsessed with knitting that I can't think about anything else, and other periods I can't go a day without sewing a couple seams. I craft because I must.

inspiration

I am influenced not only by my friends, the media, and popular culture, but also by the obscure, offbeat, and unexpected, such as a delicate pastry or the

colors in a business logo. I am easily drawn in by color (the brighter the better) and pattern, and inspiration also comes in the form of dreams or visions. These visions incubate in my head, and if I don't try to create them in tangible forms, I go a little crazy. A couple months ago, for example, I saw a small messenger tote bag I liked, but the available colors weren't to my taste. I contemplated trying to make a similar bag but discarded the idea, figuring it would be too complicated. A few days later, I awoke in the middle of the night with a picture of the bag in my brain. I couldn't get back to sleep because my brain started dissecting the pieces of the bag, trying to figure out how to build it. This happened on several different occasions, and once I actually got up and started drawing out the pattern. These visions, as strong as they are, are also fleeting and can dissipate if I don't quickly get to them.

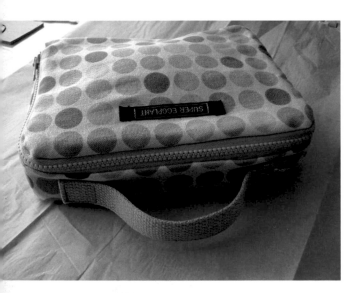

Above and Left: More of Mariko's unique bags.

Opposite: It may be in the basement, but she's got two sewing machines!

workspace

In the past, I have set up my sewing machine wherever it fit. I lived in Japan for a year and borrowed a sewing machine, which I promptly set up on an ironing board. It was quite a challenge trying to sew a fully lined trench coat while holding the ironing board steady!

We recently moved, so I am still working on making my workspace my own. Our house, in need of much renovation, is in a state of transition, so in this spirit I have established my workspace. It went from the second story to the basement, a space I initially refused to consider for my crafting space. It's all about transition, right? My current work area shares space with a treadmill and a guest bed. I have two regular sewing machines, one a new Janome 6500 and the other an Elna Super manufactured circa 1970. I also have a Bernina serger. Metal shelving units and large storage containers hold my fabric and yarn stash and my books, patterns, and notions.

This crafting thing is a compulsion. I craft because I must.

Summer Top

Directions on Page 148

about the project

Although I've tried to broaden my horizons, I find myself compelled to sew garments and bags. I have decided to share this uncontrollable passion with a pattern offering for you. It's a little summer top that is quite versatile: you can use a variety of fabrics, from cotton knit to silk to quilting cotton; you can embellish it with ribbons or buttons or sequins; and you can use contrasting fabric or even ribbon for the straps.

This pattern is unusual, because instead of telling you exactly what pieces to cut, I'm giving you instructions to create a shirt based off one you already own. It's always difficult to tell if a given pattern will fit you well, but this method ensures you get your favorite fit. I hope you enjoy it and that it inspires you to create a whole wardrobe.

Myra Masuda

Location: Honolulu, Hawaii   **Occupation:** Civil Engineer   **Age:** 30-Something

Areas of Interest: Soft Toys, Purses, Amigurumi   **Website:** http://mylittlemochi.typepad.com/

why i create

I have no formal training in art or design, but I learned to sew from an early age and crafting has always felt natural and brings me great joy and satisfaction. When I go through long periods where I'm not able to do something creative, I can get pretty cranky. So crafting is a way for me to recharge. I don't have a logical reason for why it's so important to me and what drives me to do it other than an overwhelming urge and a need to create. Making things just makes me happy.

I love handcrafted things and the intimacy in the evidence of a human hand. You see less and less handwork in our modern-day lives, and we usually buy what we need because we don't have the time or sometimes even the knowledge to make it. Handcrafting helps me reconnect to a slower time when people valued their possessions and didn't just throw them away when they broke.

Both of my parents are the children of Japanese immigrants who came to Hawaii to work in the plantations, and there wasn't a lot of money when they were growing up. Since they had so little, they were forced to be resourceful, and everything was saved, reused or re-invented for different uses. Care and workmanship was taken with everyday items, for they had to be made to last. Often when you needed something you had to make one or learn to do without.

My grandmother couldn't afford to buy my mother a lot of clothing but she allowed her to purchase as much fabric as she wanted to sew clothing for herself. My mother carried this philosophy over to me with crafting as well, as I was given almost free rein at the hobby and fabric stores but rarely taken to the toy store for purchases. I inherited from her a value and appreciation for the handmade and a can-do approach to making things.

My parents fostered a creative life for me early on and my childhood was jammed with sewing lessons, baking, weekly trips to the hobby and fabric stores, bi-weekly trips to the library in search of craft books, and lots and lots of craft projects. I first learned to sew on an old push pedal Singer sewing machine lent to us by a family friend and I spent more time pushing the pedals of that sewing machine than on the pedals of any bike.

Growing up I sewed clothes for myself, bags for school, and even my shorts for physical education classes. While my brothers were outside playing, I'd spend hours inside surrounded by piles of fabric scraps, making clothes for my Barbie dolls or drawing sketches of dresses.

My mother was also an elementary school teacher, and like most primary school teachers she was extremely resourceful and full of fun projects and ideas. I have vivid memories of a project when I was about eight. My mom took two old cream colored flat sheets, laid them out on the living room floor and then had me lie down flat on my back on top of the sheets. Then she outlined my body and head with a pen, sewed the two sheets together along the outline, cut it, stuffed it, and created a life size doll of me. I got to draw on the face, sew on some yarn hair and dress my new "friend" in my clothing. I loved this project, it was exciting and fun because she didn't tell me what we were going to do, but just let the project reveal itself to me.

I inherited a value and appreciation for the handmade.

Opposite: Myra's tiny dolls embody cuteness.

Below: A little elephant with her littler elephant.

In many ways that's how I still craft today. I don't really have a clear picture of what my end product will look like, but I enjoy the process of seeing an idea come to life on my sewing table. And when I'm done I get that same feeling of having a new friend all over again.

I tend to make small things for a couple of reasons. I work full time and have a young son, so I don't have a lot of free time to craft. I'm also impatient and become obsessed with finishing projects all in one sitting. So right now for me small projects are attainable and manageable. But I have hopes that in the future I'll have more time to tackle larger projects.

I'm constantly thinking about projects and make it a point to never leave home without a sketchbook. A lot of ideas come to me when I'm driving home in traffic. Often I'll be sketching at red lights and jotting down whatever comes to mind.

I've never fully learned the fine art of time management. Before I had my son, I really didn't have an understanding of time. It seemed never ending and looking back now I realize I wasted a lot of it. Now I try to make the most of my free moments and always take advantage of any crafting

opportunities that arise, and it's actually made me more productive. But it's still a struggle finding time to create. I like to work late at night after everyone has gone to sleep, and I have the house to myself. During these times I'm able to get into an almost Zen meditative state and have an inexplicable urge to forego much needed sleep and instead focus on a project even if it's a little stuffed animal made to please only me.

inspiration

Inspiration is everything to the creative spirit, and I find ideas come to me from everyday life, and especially from my son. Having a child in the house has to be a creative boost for anyone, just by the things they say and do. I love being surrounded by kids things – toys, picture books, crayons, tiny clothing. And when it's all strewn about I find creative inspiration in the chaos. Even something as small (and painful) as stepping on a plastic elephant may spark an idea.

Above: A sweet Amigurumi bunny.

Left: Goldilocks and friends.

My son helps me to see with new eyes the creative opportunities that are around and fully within reach. He is full of imagination and can find fun in the most mundane things and make anything come alive for him. I'm constantly stumbling upon wonderful vignettes he's created with his toys. An artfully arranged puppy intensely reading a book on bugs in the hall or a serious huddled mass of zoo animals engaged in a secret meeting on the bathtub. He shows me that even the most practical everyday things can have personality and be fun.

Reading books with my son is another creative inlet. I inherited a lot of 1950s and 60s children's books from my mother's teaching days and these are the books my son and I both gravitate to. We spend hours pouring through these books and cherish them even though many are worn and falling apart. Something about the work of illustrators of this era – the bold use of colors, and the often witty and humorous style of their art is deeply appealing and inspiring to me.

Above: Exploring new worlds can be fun.

Below: But watch out for those space monsters!

workspace

We have a tiny house, and for years my craft space was the living room floor. I would sew on the floor with my sewing machine set on a small ten-inch-high folding table and push the pedal with my thigh. My supplies and notions were strewn all over the house and setting up and breaking down this "space" whenever I wanted to make something wasted precious crafting time.

Several months ago, we did some creative re-organizing around the house and freed up a spare room for me to use as a craft room. I've always dreamed of having a workspace where I could be surrounded by things that inspire me and have all of my supplies in a central location. After years of crafting on the floor, just having a large clear work table seems like a luxury to me. So having an entire room dedicated to crafting really is a dream come true.

I borrowed an old kitchen table from my mother-in-law and my husband helped make and install some bookcases and display shelves for my supplies and fabric.

My space is still very much a work in progress, but I'm already in love with it and look forward to any opportunity I get to spend time there. . I've always placed comfort and function over style so it's a cluttered but comfy room. I love collections and groupings of things and although I'm not very good at putting artful displays together, just seeing things I love around me is inspiring and makes me happy.

Below: A space of one's own is a dream come true.

Opposite: Bowls of goodies.

Elephant Pouch

Directions on Page 150

about the project

I don't wear a lot of makeup, but I never leave the house without lipstick and some blotting papers. I used to just throw the duo into my purse, but after losing them amongst the clutter in my bag one too many times, I decided to make a little pouch to house them.

I had purchased a bag of linen scraps from a local dress designer's remnant sale and this seemed like the perfect project for them. I experimented with a couple of different dart-less versions, until I arrived at this pouch. The darts give it enough room to easily hold my lipstick and blotters, and even an additional lipstick.

It really is a simple project, and can easily be adapted for other animal faces or done without a face at all. And I smile every time I reach into my purse for my lipstick and pull out this little guy.

Sarah Neuburger

Location: Irmo, South Carolina   **Occupation:** Craft Entrepreneur   **Age:** 29

Areas of Interest: Paper Goods, Housewares, Original Artwork   **Website:** http://www.thesmallobject.com/

why i create

This is one of those questions that seems bigger than life, like why are we here, is Pluto a planet, is Coke really refreshing. And the truth of the matter is I have no idea, but I do know if I didn't create, there would be no point in being here. You know, it's just one of those things like apples and peanut butter, parks and picnics, music and driving. Who knows why – it just came to be, and they are so perfect together. So while I can't answer why I do it, I do know how it's come to pass. I know with great certainty that it is easier to choose a path when it's lined with a few good cheerleaders, and I've been most blessed in this regard.

Let me introduce you to the likes of Ms. Celeste. In high school, I made a painting of a nude woman sitting with her legs crossed. I named her Ms. Celeste. It was a pretty large painting for somebody my age – about four feet tall and three feet wide – matted out even a foot or two larger in all directions. And it caused a ruckus at my high school because my teacher entered it in a national art contest, which was really much more a gold star game between art teachers than about us, the students. Word on the street was the judges for that contest didn't know what to do with it either, since I shouldn't have had any access to a nude model at that age, and her figure was by no means cover girl material. I also had to have a meeting with the principal over what would happen if the painting was actually displayed

at this contest and whether or not the school should be labeled (which was customary) and associated with such a scandal. The details, ridiculous as they are, don't really matter but what does matter is my father's reaction. I was to have the meeting with the principal on my own with a bulleted list of points which my father and I had compiled and debated in advance. It was my job to stick up for what I had done and stick by Ms. Celeste to the teeth. For a good solid year anyone, absolutely anyone, who came in to the house was shown this painting, usually after the guest had just finished their dinner and was given the cliff notes to its story, all told by my father as he gazed at her with such pride. She would be propped up on the edge of the dining room table, looming down over our friends, barely missing the chandelier and seeming oh so out of place among the leftover pork chops and smashed green beans. The point being my father fell madly for Ms. Celeste, and the pride I felt in having created her was a high like none other. Sadly, or perhaps appropriately, Ms. Celeste was later thrown away in a weird twist of events by my mother, through no fault of her own.

Now my mother is another story. She makes everything and always seems to have it all ready to go. From creating a card catalog of the contents of our freezer (which we had to "check out" before eating) to sewing up a new line of summer trousers each year, she did it all. And she always had a space of her own to create it all in, stuffed with perfectly penned labeled boxes full of potential. She made me blankets, dolls, curtains with matching wallpaper, embroidered Holly Hobby pictures to hang over my bed, painted wood in my initials. The activity was so constant that it seems so unnatural to not do these things. I mean, are there really people who don't own a Dremel, jigsaw, embroidery machine, glass etcher, pleater, staple gun, Styrofoam cutter, assortment of foam balls, an attic full of fabric scraps, oil paints or a linoleum cutter? Truly, there must not be! My world had it all on hand for most every project and a mother who was always game. No matter what, handmade is always better, there's no question about it.

If I didn't create, there would be no point in being here.

Opposite: Little Small Clothespin People.

Below: Interesting paper gooding

So sorry kids, it just feels right and I don't decide to do it, I just do it. I make things because it seems downright impossible to have it any other way. We all create, make up our own worlds, have our own fantasies and spend hours wondering about this or that. There is no separation and there is no real reason. It is my everyday and has always been that way since the dawn of my time. My grandmother was a shoe designer. My other Granma could bake like nobody's business (and I have eaten myself silly sick off her deliciousness on more then one occasion). My father was an architect student and hopeless romantic. My Granpa had a wood shop in his backyard shaped like a barn which churned out napkin holders and snowmen holding holiday greetings. My mother is still the one who has everything on hand. There was no single event that made me create. Perhaps creativity is just in us and mine happened to be supported from the get go. I am lucky enough to know at my core there could be no other way for me and for the map of my course to be dotted with tiny jumping people holding pom-poms, with new recruits picked up along the way. And each of those good sports means the world to me.

inspiration

I feel on top of my world right now, running my own little cottage industry of handmade wares and original artwork. How this all came into being and what inspired it all happened with one single order. I remember so very clearly, way back upon a time when I ordered my very first item from an incredibly talented person selling her wares through her very own online store. It was Saelee Oh, and I happened across her site by accident. I recall so vividly that magic happened the day the envelope arrived with my purchase inside. It seemed so average: a plain white envelope with my name scrawled on the front. But inside, there was a handwritten note about the weather which wasn't important, but what was so important to me is that she referenced where I lived

– she noticed. It was such a small simple gesture that moved my world an inch closer to sunnyside up. And inside were free stickers I hadn't even ordered but were so flippin' beautiful. (I still have one unused and one that quickly became the centerpiece of my sketchbook cover.) The envelope I even still have, tucked away knowing it forever changed me in some way. Never again would I buy my gifts from Target, cool as they are. Never again would I spend my money at some place that didn't care. (Of course, I have, but that day I was on top of the world and I knew that when a handmade option was available, that was what I would choose.)

After Saelee Oh, I discovered there was already a whole network of artist/crafters selling their wares online and the whole experience of buying from them reminded me of the days when you'd sit down to your brown paper bag lunch, your name scrawled on the front, and you're so hungry you can't wait to see what's inside. You're just giddy to open it, partly because you want what's inside so bad but also because carefully unfolding the top and peering down into its contents is so incredible. And you open it up, and it is full of deliciousness, each individually wrapped and bagged with such care. And then there would be a napkin with a note written on it that could say anything from the simple "I love you" to the punchline of some funny joke we had talked about the night before. It was the best experience and that was the kind of energy I wanted to put back out there. I make things hoping that it makes that connection again. It is that moment that inspires me endlessly. I want nothing more than more magic spilling open in your mailbox and many more moments filled with good cheer.

workspace

For whatever reason, I went right from undergraduate to graduate school. And I was so very excited to finally get a studio space in a building with huge soaring windows and be surrounded by countless inspiring folks. Truly, this was what I looked forward to most about the next two years of school. Funny thing happened though. I never worked there! I couldn't do it. I wanted my couch and my cats around; I always ended up needing something I didn't cart down to the studio, which was endlessly frustrating. Plus, I hated having to run down the hall for a drink or having to listen to the music in the next room or the mumbled conversations of others. I wanted to be home.

At this point, my workspace is here, there and everywhere. My mother, besides being a jack of all trades, is also an organizational freak. I, too, compartmentalize everything and while it can get messy along the way, I can pack it all up in two minutes flat. It may seem impossible, but trust me I can do it. The actual "workspace" of my house has a large wrap-around desk with shelves for all my bins. Though truth be told, there are paints, paper, scissors and glue in the kitchen drawers; a dresser full of pencils, erasers, sketchbooks and cameras in my bedroom; saws and silkscreening supplies in the garage; and a power cord for my laptop in most rooms in the house. I like to get around. Suffice to say, my living space is my workspace. By now, I realize I can have it no other way, it surrounds me and reminds me and, I'm most certain, loves me.

Opposite: One of Sarah's Stick People Portraits.

Above: An unusual pincushion.

Left: Sarah's desk, safe at home.

Fabric Basket

Directions on Page 152

about the project

This basket is the ideal place for all your desktop clutter, because you can throw in your stuff and cinch up the top. My workspace is basically a sea of container islands, each holding their own bins of organized clutter. It makes me feel calm, and yet I don't feel like everything is too neat to mess up.

This basket is also perfect for on-the-go crafting from one space to another. I tend to move from the desk to the bed to the sofa to the front porch, so this will stick with you no problem. There is plenty of interfacing in this pattern, so it holds its shape quite well.

Tania Ho

Location: Lisbon, Portugal   **Occupation:** Computer Science Engineer   **Age:** 32

Areas of Interest: Book Covers, Pouches, Needle Cases   **Website:** http://chocolateachuva.blogspot.com/

why i create

My love for crafting comes from childhood, I guess. I still clearly remember one of my favourite books from when I was a child: it was called "My Learn to Sew Book," by Janet Barber. Oh, it had wonderful projects, especially in the eyes of a 10 year old, and I particularly liked the rag doll project so much that I tried to sew one several times, but much to my disappointment, it never came out as I expected.

Then in high school, I went through a "I want to sew my own clothes" phase, which – thanks to my best friend's mum – actually turned out quite acceptably. She taught me everything I know about sewing, and to this day I can still remember all her advice. Then for a long number of years, I didn't do any crafting at all, either because I didn't have the time or just didn't have any real motivation.

So it was with a bit of a surprise that sometime last year I was overcome with this desire to start sewing again. Inspired by all the crafty blogs and the beautiful handmade things I saw everyday, I decided it was time to start using the old sewing machine once more. I didn't have any clear project on my mind, just an urge to try to create something, so I went fabric shopping and came home with a small stash, including some pieces of suede that had caught my attention. When I looked at them at the shop, my first thought was "I bet that would be

perfect for making a book cover." Now, why would that thought even occur to me? Well, first because I'm an avid reader, and I'm never without a book inside my bag, and they usually end up a bit scruffy on the edges. And second because I had just come back from a vacation to Italy, where I had seen the most wonderful leather book covers for sale at the San Lorenzo market. Because they were expensive, I had only purchased one, but now my mind was wondering whether I could sew one myself. And that's how it all started actually – and now, almost 200 book covers and other items later, I can say that crafting is definitely a huge part of my life now and is here to stay.

My main problem (and I think every crafter's problem) is not having enough time to do all the projects I want. So many times I have wished the day had more than twenty four hours. I have one box full of fabric pieces that I keep saving for myself, in the hopes of someday having time to make that bag or whatever item I had imagined.

Although sewing will always be my passion – I just love working with fabrics - recently I've also taken on knitting as well. I found out that it relaxes me a lot, and gives me a totally different satisfaction than sewing. When sewing, I can be much more creative and never know quite what the end result will be, but they're usually quick projects with almost immediate gratification. What I love about knitting is the opposite: watching the project grow, little by little, the feeling of the yarn in my hands, and at the end the sense of achievement is so huge that I just feel like I've completed the marathon every time.

I guess the main reason why I craft is because I never tire of that sense of accomplishment when I finish an item, whether it's a small or big project. I always try to use my best ideas and effort whenever I'm making something, but when the idea actually turns out into the reality I had envisioned, I'm still surprised how it all worked out.

Crafting is a huge part of my life and is here to stay.

Opposite: Tania's trademark book covers.

Below: Serious discussion between pals.

inspiration

I get inspired by a lot of things around me, from places I visit, advertisements or people I pass on the street who are wearing something I like, to something eye-catching I see in a store somewhere. I have a small pocket notebook I carry in my purse, and I scribble down notes and drawings of things I've seen or ideas I've had and don't want to forget.

Of course, one of my main inspiration sources are all these amazing crafty blogs and sites that keep appearing more and more everyday. I'm constantly surprised to find out about this or that talented crafter, and my list on bloglines keeps growing all the time (and I never imagined I would spend so much time reading blogs – or when I'm in a hurry, just looking at the photos – but I never go a day without).

Magazines and books are also a source, especially Japanese or French ones. Not that I understand what's written, but what they say about an image being worth a thousand words usually works for me in this case. I try not to buy so many but sometimes it is hard to resist.

I'm lucky because I have so many friends that share this passion for crafting as well, so we exchange ideas, patterns and advice quite often. And because I make a lot of items on demand, my clients are also a huge source of inspiration to me.

workspace

Well, to be truly honest, I don't really have a fixed workspace. Because our house is so small, my workspace is actually wherever there's free space, usually the kitchen table or the sitting room floor. And since I have two cats in the house, and one of their favourite games is to steal whatever small objects I'm working with, sometimes this can be a bit of a problem.

It took me a long time to organize my materials in a satisfactory way, but for now I'm happy with how they are. Of course, what started as a small stash of fabrics has now grown to a huge pile, and fills almost seven big cardboard boxes (oh, and the yarn stash which is neatly hidden under the sofa). We are planning to move to a bigger place soon, so I have plans for a crafting room of my own, but apart from a large desk and a big bookcase to hold all my crafting tools and materials, I don't really have an idea of a dream workspace in my head yet.

Below: A personalized quilt.

Opposite: Materials sorted out and ready to go.

Book Cover

Directions on Page 154

about the project

I've always been an obsessive reader, so it seemed natural to start making covers to protect my books when I'm carrying them everywhere with me. There are several bookcover styles and patterns out there, but this was inspired in some Japanese covers I've seen and although they're the most practical – you can read the book without having to take the cover out – one cover will only fit one particular book size. So if you're like me, you'll be needing dozens of these covers, one for each size!

This project will fit a small regular paperback book, but it's very easy to adjust its size to fit any other book. Just add more width or height to the pattern according to the book dimensions, bearing in mind that you should always add at least 1/4" extra to each side to account for fabric turning and its thickness.

Tania Howells

Location: Toronto, Canada   **Occupation:** Illustrator, Librarian   **Age:** 31

Areas of Interest: Silkscreening, Felting, Knitting   **Website:** http://tania.blogs.com/

why i create

There is an absolute comfort and joy in closing the front door, surrounding yourself in your favourite materials and making something for the pure fun of it.

As a child, the cupboard by the telephone was my creative source. It was where I kept all and any things I needed to make stuff. I would often just open the door and rummage through the junk for the fun of it, finding such pleasure in just the materials themselves. Sometimes I would be inspired enough to start a project, or be spurred on to collect other things from around the house to keep inside for later ideas. My creativity was never discouraged or frowned upon, and I am so fortunate for that.

I remember a time at some stage of childhood where I was consumed by the idea of painting pebbles with animals on them. My father, always one to join in on a good project, took the dog and me to the river to find just the right stones. We gathered up a few and took them home to the kitchen table and went to work. I still to this day have the lady bug stone I painted on that afternoon, as well as one that says simply "dad". I also remember a twig whittling phase where I would spend afternoons in the back yard, carving twigs from our willow tree. My parents were less enthusiastic about that one, as it involved a sharp knife, but I did okay. There were of course the "stapling papers to make books" phase

(grade two) and the "making a puppet worm with some sticks and foam "phase (grade five) as well as the requisite Lego villages, rock collections, sticker albums, stamp collections, and endless drawings.

I went to an art high school where I painted big messy paintings about nothing at all. I always had romantic fantasies of becoming a famous Painter! Capital P! I then went to an art college where those fantasies generally faded. I took no painting courses at all. My favourites classes had names like "intro to wood", "enamelling", "hand building in clay" and "silver smithing" – crafty classes.   I was always most interested in making things that regular people could relate to and have in their homes. People like me who had bills to pay, dishes to wash and everyday life to contend with. The lofty ideals of the fine art world left me absolutely cold. I took to making small wood boxes with silly scenes in them that people would buy to put in their kitchens or kids rooms.

After college, I adopted the title "freelance illustrator" and took to trying to convince various magazines to hire me to draw pictures for money. I have never been very good at the convincing people part, but enough magazines have joined in on the deal to satisfy me.

I have always felt both craft and illustration are somewhat looked down upon by "fine artists". It is a funny hierarchy, and I have lately given up caring about it. It is here in the land between fine art and fine craft that I feel most at home, just making stuff.

Most unexpected is how my starting a web log in 2004 has fuelled my love for craft even more. It was there that I discovered other women's crafty blogs and was instantly inspired. When I began my own blog I was amazed at the supportive, inclusive non-competitive community I had fallen into without even realizing. It was a feeling I never felt throughout art school or in the art community, which always felt to me to be so cut-throat, harsh and unfriendly. Having

My creativity was never discouraged or frowned upon.

Opposite: Painted stones from Tania's childhood.

Below: A 3D collage made from Tania's illustrations.

This Page: Tania's inspiration board is a collection of bits and pieces from other artists.

Opposite: Vintage teacups provide inspiration.

this supportive community now means an always available sounding board for new ideas, a wonderful cheering committee for ideas and a place to showcase works in progress.

Currently, crafting for me means time set aside as a savoured treat- a break from the busyness of the world to just indulge and make something for the pure pleasure of it. Sometimes it is about being struck with a fun project idea to later sell on my web site or just an idea for an item I will keep for myself. It is the joy of learning to knit, something I never dreamed I would be able to figure out, and then seeing my own progress as I am able to take on more and more complicated projects. It is the surprised satisfaction of making a little thing for myself, only to find that there is a market and other people will buy it. It is the amazed feeling when you produce something or other, post about it on the blog and receive wonderful positive feedback from people all over the world! This last part truly amazes me- it is the one of most surprising and fun parts of my life today.

inspiration

Inspiration comes in all shapes and forms and often in ordinary moments of my days. The one thing all the contributors in this book have in common is our participation in the online crafting weblog community, and I get boundless inspiration from all the work I see there. On a more personal level, the littlest things are what usually inspire me. Right in front of my house, inspiration might be seeing an icy frost pattern on a sewer grate, a flock of pigeons doing a loop de loop, a funny hand-painted sign in the butcher shop across the street or seeing a mum and baby walk by. In and around my city, a walk to work through the park always makes me feel better and more inspired, seeing interesting things in shop windows, noticing what clothes people are wearing and having a nice cup of tea along the way. Sometimes, even kissing my fiancé inspires me! If I am in a particularly good

mood, a kiss from him lights all kinds of images in my brain of things I want to make. That's how I know he is right for me! I always try and look at ordinary things from new angles and try to remember not to take them for granted. Over the years I have kept scrap books full of snips from magazines of all sorts of inspiring images. I look through these books regularly to bring me back to a sense of myself and of what I like. All the pictures, chosen by me, have collectively created a sort of safety zone, a place where I am reminded of the richness and beauty in the world and of what specifically inspires me. I sometimes also keep lists of things I encounter during my days.

I also have the good fortune to work part time in a design library, where there are a number of great magazine subscriptions and interesting books. Also

things that inspire me:

-bundles of sticks

-toast and jam

-50's patterned saucers

-a lovely cool summer

-dim sum

-cute stickers

-swimming at Sandbanks Beach

-fireflies

-handsome men on bicycles

-winter comfort foods

-buying new shampoo

-lemons in a nice bowl

-skating on the Rideau Canal

-nice cup of tea

-fat fluffy snowflakes

Below: Inspiring children's books from Tania's collection.

there are files and files of images, which have been compiled from the 1950's onward and are used as reference material. I always love to look through them, as often I will find something of interest in the most unexpected places.

workspace

I work in a north facing room above a main street in a 3 bedroom apartment that I share with my fiancé. I have a nice long folding table under the window as my desk and beside that, my computer table where I work on a new IMAC G5 that I love. I surround myself with all sorts of books, knick knacks, an inspiration board and art supplies. My cats are usually close by, snoring under the desk or on a chair. I always have music or the radio on and usually have a cup of tea on the go too. I tend to work in here on weekday mornings and go to my job in the afternoons. I do anything from working on illustration jobs, sketching out new ideas and thoughts, packaging orders from my web store, exposing new silkscreens, paying bills and of course answering e-mails and updating my blog or web site! The table in the studio is usually covered in piles of paper that I tidy up periodically as well as pens, CDs, inks and brushes, a day timer and to do list notebook and any number of bits and bobs I find inspiring at that moment. The only part of my crafty endeavours that does not happen here is the fabric part of them. I sew and silkscreen things in the back room of this apartment- a brick unheated addition which has wonderful south facing light. I am lucky to have this extra space for doing the messy or cumbersome parts of projects because there really is not room in my studio. My fiancé and I have just bought a new house, and I know I will miss the spacious working environment I have been enjoying here for the last seven or eight years!

Opposite, Top: Illustration by Tania Howells.

Opposite, Bottom: The contents of Tania's sewing box.

Needle Case

Directions on Page 156

about the project

For this case I used the denim from a too-long jean skirt and a machine stitched version of one of my birds that was a gift from a blog reader. The inside fabric was also a gift and the white fabric was thrifted. I printed it with a silkscreen of black birds and then stamp decorated it further. You can embellish it any way you like - with iron-on transfers, stamps, patterns made with different color threads sewn on, stencils, dying, quilting - whatever you might like to try.

A lot of the case is patched together from smaller pieces and you can feel free to use scraps of different prints or colors to add up and make the correct sized pieces. Don't be afraid to experiment! Remember this is not something you will be wearing, so it can be a bit more wild if you feel like playing.

Zakka-Style Pouch

Shibori Felted Piece

Materials

- 1 Skein Superbulky Pure Wool (www.handpaintedyarn. com) in colourway 'Paris Night'
- 6.5mm needles
- Selection of small pebbles or beads
- Squares of plastic food film cut into approximately 10cm squares
- Small rubber bands

Tension: 14st/19rows = 10cm square

Any pure wool will work, but it must be 100% wool. Single ply wools tend to be softer and felt more densely.
Cast on 100 st. Knit in stockinette stitch for 20 rows. Cast off loosely.

Place a bead to the wrong side of the knitted piece, push it up, and cover the resulting bobble on the right side with a piece of film. Secure in place with a rubber band. The cling film ensures that this part of the knit will not felt in the machine, giving some textural difference to the piece. Ensure the rubber band holding the bead and film in place is secure. Continue placing the beads along the length of the knit in random patterns and groupings (odd number groupings work best visually). Don't go too close to edges, though, leaving about 2cm border if possible.

Place beaded piece in an old pillowcase, and close it by pinning or tying the top in a knot. Add this to the washing machine along with items to help agitation: old sneakers, tennis balls, a towel etc. NOTE: Some yarn can lose a lot of dye – if you are in any doubt about the colourfastness of the wool you are felting, please use old pillowcases, towels and objects in the washing machine. Add a small dollop of wool wash detergent. Put the machine on the hottest water setting and set the machine. Check on progress every 10 minutes till you have the desired amount of felting. This piece, in my machine, took 25 minutes. Remove from machine and rinse thoroughly with cold water and hang to dry. You can block it if you feel it needs shaping, but the piece will pull into shape when sewn. Once dry, remove film, rubber bands and beads/pebbles.

Knitted Pouch Bottom

Materials

- 1 50g ball of Rowan 4ply Cotton, colour 112
- A set of four 3mm (US 2) double pointed needles

Tension: 13st/19rows = 5cm

Other wool combinations can be used, however cotton gives a rigidity and tightness of weave which is good for a pouch bottom. You can always go down a needle size to get a tighter knit as well.
Cast on 34 st to each of 3 needles – 102st total.
Join yarn for working in the round, ensuring stitches are not twisted across the 3 needles. Knit every row until the piece measures 5cm from cast on edge.
Begin shaping:
R1 – Needle 1: K1, K2tog, K to last 3 st. K2tog, K1. Repeat across remaining 2 needles.
R2 – Knit.
Repeat R1 and R2 till 16st remain on each needle (48st total) ending with a R2.
Each row – R1 (decrease each row) till 3 st remain on each needle (9 total).

Cut yarn, leaving a 30cm tail. Thread a wool needle, and starting with the next st in turn, thread the needle through each st, drawing the tail yarn through as you slip the stitches off the needle, and in so doing pulling the stitches close with the yarn to close the bottom of the pouch. Tie the yarn on the wrong side to secure, and weave in ends thoroughly before trimming excess yarn away.
Lightly steam press.

Pouch Body

Materials

- 1 White linen napkin
- Scraps of coordinating fabrics
- Ribbon for the tie.
- Embroidery thread and needle. DMC Colour 321.
- 3 buttons
- Tracing paper
- Fabric pen which fades

Step One

Measure the circumference of the Knitted Pouch Bottom and add 1.5cm (gives a 3/4cm seam allowance). This piece measures 50cm.

Step Two

The Pouch is composed of the base pieces in Fig. 1 on page 129. Cut these pieces from your fabric.

Step Three

Once you have cut out your fabric strips, start piecing them together. The fabric strips shown are pieced together in the following way:

Material A – Single Piece

Material B/C – 2 Pieces of coordinating fabrics sewn side-by-side with 1/2cm seam allowance and trimmed to 50cm so the pieces are uneven in width.

Step Four

Piecing together:

a) With right sides together, pin the Shibori felt to top of Material B/C. Sew in place, taking it slowly with the felt in the machine. I suggest overpinning the knitted piece to the material to stop it moving. The felt will be soft to sew, and the needle should move through easily.

b) With right sides together, pin the Shibori to the bottom of Material A, and again sew in place.

c) With *wrong* sides together, pin the top of Material A to the linen napkin. This seam will be a French Seam. Sew very close to the edge – about 1-2mm from the edge in a straight line. Press the seam flat to one side. With right sides together now, sew the seam with 1/2cm allowance, and press flat. This will give you a neat, hidden, finished seam, and the linen won't fray visibly.

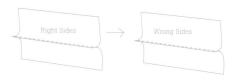

d) Press the seam to one side and ensure it sits flat.

e) Press open other seams as best you can with the Shibori thickness.

Step Five

Turn over the top of the linen napkin to create the recess for the ribbon tie. First fold and iron down about 10mm (towards the wrong side), then fold and iron down another 2cm. Sew across, close to the edge.

Step Six

Press finished material piece flat, ready for Sashiko embroidery.

Step Seven

Divide your DMC embroidery thread into 3-strand lots. With a fabric pen, mark out a squiggle circle design onto linen.

With running stitch, embroider along the lines, ensuring you follow a 3mm/2mm stitch/gap length ratio (this is what makes it Sashiko). Sew on 3 buttons to create highlight.

Step Eight

With wrong sides together, pin the side edges of the material together to form a tube. French seam as before, pressing carefully at each stage. Ensure you only sew to the start of the top hem foldover – it needs to remain open for the ribbon. Turn tube inside out.

Step Nine

Place knitted pouch bottom inside main material tube (right sides together), with bottom of tube edge lining up with top cast on edge of pouch. Pin (overpin if possible) in place and ensure knitting sits flat against the material – it is fairly pliable so should be able to be manipulated easily to allow this to happen.

Step Ten

Slowly and carefully sew through both layers, checking constantly the material and knit positions. It is a good idea to do this by hand.

Step Eleven

Turn the whole piece right way round and press gently.

Step Twelve

Using approximately 1m of ribbon, thread this through the hem to create a drawstring closure to the pouch. Trim ribbon to desired length – I like to leave about a 20cm tail at either end. I leave the hemmed opening unfinished – with the idea it will fray and wear, giving the pouch some roughness and life.

Step Fourteen

Fill pouch with knitting and find a nice café and order a coffee and some cake!

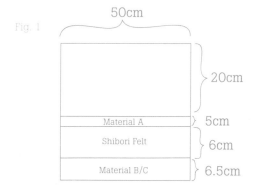

Fig. 1

(Knit Bottom Goes Here)

Quilted Throw

Materials

- 2 yards light yellow cotton
- 2 yards medium yellow cotton
- 2.5 yards dark yellow cotton
- multiple 1/4 yards of patterned cotton
- 1/4 yard white cotton
- For the quilt back, several pieces of varying yardage, pieced together to make a 63" x 61" back
- 63" x 61" piece of quilt batting
- Water-soluble marking pen for fabric

To replicate the details on this piece you will also need a sewing machine that has a darning foot for free motion quilting, or the ability to lower your feed dogs.

Step One

Cut the three shades of yellow cotton into 9 1/2" lengths. Cut the lengths into different widths and lay them out in rows which measure 61" wide (don't forget your seam allowances!). I start by creating one row, usually with about 3-4 different pieces of yellow pieced together. When I am happy with that size, I set it aside and then make the other rows the same way, with different yellows pieced together building the quilt by rows as I go. There are 7 rows in the quilt approximately 9 1/2" wide, which includes a 1/4 inch seam allowance. I also take a lot of digital photos while I'm planning, so I can refer to them when I start sewing. Sew the strips into rows, but don't sew together the rows just yet.

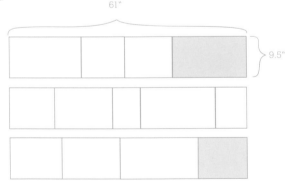

Step Two

Using a water-soluble pen, draw ovals in different sizes on the white cotton. Cut out, leaving about 1/2" extra around the marked line. Cut tabs to the marked line. Remove the line with water. Do this before you iron, or it might not wash off, and iron all the tabs toward the center, pressing carefully so there are no sharp edges. (Fig. 1)

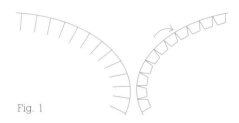

Fig. 1

Step Three

Pin the shapes to your quilt, playing with the placement over the rows. You can match the look of mine or change them around. When you have placed all of the shapes, take a digital photo for reference.

Step four

Now this part is pretty organic. Depending on where your shapes are, you will need to stitch some rows together before you machine appliqué the shapes on. It is easier to work on as few rows as possible, because it's hard to maneuver a large top through your machine. So trace around the placement of all the shapes with your water-soluble pen and take them off (keep track of what oval goes where in a system that works for you) then stitch together the rows needed to make a background for the shapes.

Step Five

Pin the shapes on the rows where you marked and using a tiny zigzag in white, stitch the oval to the top. Use a lot of pins, especially on the big shapes because they like to pucker.

Step Six

Do this combination of stitching rows together and the stitching on of the shapes until all the shapes are used up. Add any free-motion "drawing" in a contrasting thread at this point if you want to. I just wing it and start drawing, but you can also draw something out first with your water-soluble pen and follow the line.

Step Seven

Now stitch any remaining rows together to make the complete top. You might only have 2-3 very large pieces left at this point.

Step Eight

Now your top is done! Square up the edges so the quilt is as true to the grain as possible.

Step Nine

Piece together the back with fabrics to make a piece large enough to be about 1" larger than the quilt top. I love to use unexpected patterns on the back, and never have enough, which is why my quilts look this way, but you can also just use one solid color.

Step Ten

Sandwich the back, batting and top together and pin like crazy starting from the center outward. The closer you pin, the less puckering you will get when you quilt. This takes a while.

Step Eleven

Machine quilt through all layers either using the design I did, which is a free handed large scallop (you need to use a free-motion setting on your machine), or you can just stitch straight rows if you like. A good rule is there should be no more than about 4" between quilting lines to prevent shifting. This will take a long time. Roll up your quilt as you go and try not to rush this part. It's hard getting a big top through your home machine, but it can be done.

Step Twelve

Make the binding by cutting 2 1/4" wide strips of yellow and piecing in contrasting fabrics if you like. Make the strip long enough to go all the way around your quilt. Iron all this in half, right sides facing out. Sew the raw edges of the binding all the way around, 1/4" from the edge.

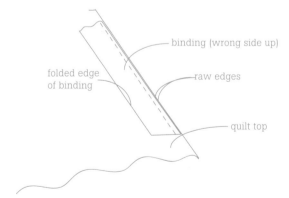

binding (wrong side up)

folded edge
of binding

raw edges

quilt top

Step Thirteen

Fold the binding over to the back of the quilt and slip stitch the fold edge to the back. This takes forever, but it is the only way I put on quilt bindings because it always looks perfect and gives you complete control. Plan on doing this while watching 2-3 movies.

slip stitch

back of quilt

Step Fourteen

Wash and dry your quilt! I never pre-wash my fabrics for quilts because I love the way they pucker up and look when they shrink and it hides bumps and imperfections.

Market Bag

Materials
½ yard Print One
1 yard Print Two
1 yard Lining Fabric
1 yard Piping
1 yard Ribbon

Notes
All seams are sewn with a ¼" seam allowance – this is built into the below measurements.

Step One
From Print One, cut the following:
A (5.5" x 19.5") x 2 (Outer Bag)
B (20" x 4") x 2 (Handles)
C (18" x 2") x 2 (Casing)

From Print Two, cut the following:
D (14" x 19.5") x 2 (Outer Bag)
E (31" x 8") x 1 (Pocket)

From your lining fabric, cut the following:
F (19" x 19.5") x 2 (Lining)

From your piping, cut the following:
G (20") x 2

From your ribbon, cut the following:
H (40") x 2

Step Two
Sew one piece A to a piece D, right sides together, sandwiching the piping (G) in between. Repeat with the other pieces A and D.

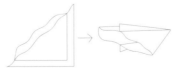

Step Three
Take the two pieces you've just created, and match them up, right sides together. Make sure the piping on either end lines up on both pieces. Pin and sew around the sides and bottom.

Step Four
With the bag still inside-out, take one corner and bring the two seams together. The corner should still be a right angle, and you should smooth out

any wrinkles. Pin it flat. Mark a line 5" across, with the centre (2.5") on the seam. Sew along this line, repeat for other corner. Cut off the extra corner fabric, remembering to leave at least ¼".

Step Five
Using the panels for the lining (F), repeat steps three and four.

Step Six
To create the handles, use the two B strips. Iron both sides in ½", then fold the strip in half and iron. Sew down the open sides, ¼" from the edge. Repeat for the second handle.

Step Seven
To create the pocket, fold piece E in half, right sides together and sew up either side. Turn it right-side-out and iron flat. Fold the finished edge up so that it falls 3" short of the unfinished edges. Sew up either side.

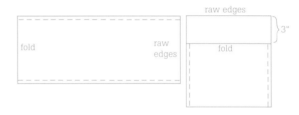

Step Eight
Turn the lining right-side-out. Lining up the edges, pin the pocket to the centre top of the lining.

Step Nine

On the outside fabric, measure six inches in from either side and use these marks to centre the handle. Pin it as shown, making sure it is not twisted. Repeat on other side for second handle. Turn this piece inside-out.

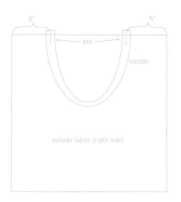

Step Ten

Place the right-side-out lining inside the outer fabric. Line up the seams on either side and pin together, making sure the raw edges are even all the way around. Sew around, leaving a 3" hole to turn piece through.

Step Eleven

Turn the entire piece right-side-out and put the lining inside the bag. Making sure the pocket is in side the bag, press the seam flat and then stitch around the top of the bag, closing your turning hole in the process. (Fig 1)

Step Twelve

Using the casing pieces (C), iron in either side ½", and tuck under and iron the short ends by ½" as well. Pin these in place, 3" from the top of the bag. Start just off centre of one handle and end just short of centre on the other side. Repeat with the second strip for the other side of the bag. Slip stitch the casing to the bag on all sides, leaving the short ends open.

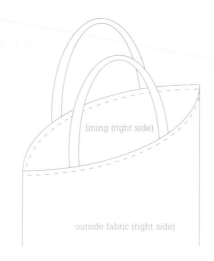

(Alternatively, you can make the casing strips wider and machine sew them to the outside of the bag after step four.)

Step Thirteen

Thread one piece of ribbon through the casing, beginning on one side of the bag and ending on the same side. Thread the second piece of ribbon through in the same fashion, but start on the opposite side of the bag. Once they're in place, either tie a knot in the ends of the ribbons or tie on a bead so the ends cannot slip back through the casing. To cinch up the bag, pull all ribbons at one and tie each pair in a bow to secure.

Fabric Scarf and Brooch

Materials
- 1 3/4 yards of fabric (if you use a different print for the front and back, you will need two 1 3/4 yard lengths)
- several scraps of coordinating fabric for the brooch
- 1 4" x 4" piece of heavy cotton canvas
- 1 button
- Sew-on pin back
- Flexible, permanent fabric glue (such as Aleene's OK To Wash-It)
- Coordinating embroidery floss

Scarf Instructions:

Step One
Open and refold your fabric so the two cut ends are together. From the fold, measure and cut a piece which is 11" wide and 31" long. You should have a piece which is 11" wide and 62" long when unfolded. Repeat for second side.

Step Two
With right sides together, pin the two pieces together, leaving a 5" hole on one of the short sides for turning. Sew around all four sides, leaving a 1/2" seam allowance, and remember to leave the turning hole open.

Step Three
Iron the seam back from the hole, clip the corners, and turn the piece right-side-out.

Step One
Press flat and slip stitch the opening closed. Your scarf is finished!

Brooch Instructions:

Step One
Choose three coordinating patterns for your brooch. From one print, cut a piece 2" x 11" (for the front). From another, cut a piece 4" x 11" (for the middle). From the third, cut a piece 5" x 5" (for the back).

Step Two
For the front piece, trim one long edge with pinking or scalloping shears. Make a running stitch along the untrimmed long side, leaving a 1/4" seam allowance.

Connect the two ends of thread and gather the fabric along the running stitch to create a tight circle. Once tightened, tie the two ends of the thread together in a knot. Arrange the pleats so it's fairly even all the way around, and set this piece aside.

ends of thread

Step Three
For the middle piece of the flower, fold the fabric in half lengthwise, and finger press along the fold.

fold

raw edges

Skipping the pinking shears, follow the same directions from step two to create another circle.

Step Four
For the back piece, trace the circle template onto your piece of fabric and cut out (see page 137 for the template). Then make 1/4" deep cuts, 1/4" apart, all around the edge of the circle. After clipping, 'rough' up the edges a bit with your fingers to give it texture.

Step Five
Stack the three flower pieces on top of each other and top with your chosen button. Sew all these pieces together, going through the holes of the button.

Step Six
Using the second circle template (also on page 137), cut out the back support from your heavy cotton canvas. Sew the pin back to the center of this piece.

Step Seven
Spread the fabric glue over the other side of the back support and press the back of your flower to it. Allow it to fully dry, and your flower brooch is finished!

Patchwork Purse

Materials

For the purse:
- Strips of fabric 10.5" wide
- Lining fabric, 10.5" x 16"
- Interfacing, or 3 to 4 pieces of plain cotton fabric, for interlining, same size as lining
- 2 buttons
- Length of cord approx 6" long
- Embroidery thread

For the corsage:
- Scraps of fabric approx 4" square
- 1 button
- brooch back/pin back

Purse
Step One
Gather together your fabric strips and when you are happy, stitch together until your piece is approximately 16" long.

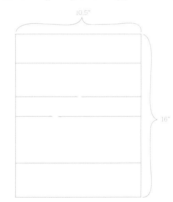

Step Two
Cut your lining and interlining fabric(s) to the same size as your patchwork.

Step Three
Put your patchwork and lining fabrics right sides together, place your interlining on the top and pin together. Stitch together, leaving a gap for turning.

Step Four
Turn right side out and stitch gap closed.

Step Five
Fold over, about 5.5" from bottom edge to make your purse shape, and then blanketstitch the sides together. Blanket stitch around remaining edges for a smart decorative finish.

Step Six
Attach a button to the front of your purse approximately 1.5" from the bottom edge, and then thread your cord through your other button and attach to the flap as shown.

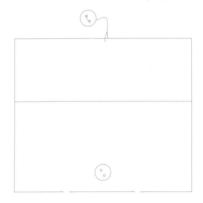

Corsage
Step One
Cut six petals and one circle from your chosen fabrics. The templates are on page 145.

Step Two
Stack all the pieces up, and stitch together through the centre of each petal, finishing off with a button.

Step Three
Sew on the brooch back and pin to your bag.

Library Tote

Materials

All measurements include seam allowances. Please remember to allow 1/4" extra for each sewn edge if you are making this bag to your own specifications.

- 2 pieces fabric for outside of bag. For this bag I used 12" wide x 15" tall. Try to choose fabric with a reasonably heavy weave for durability and strength, such as denim, corduroy, upholstery-weight cotton or linen.
- 2 pieces of contrasting fabric - using same measurements as above for inside of bag. A lightweight quilting cotton was used here.
- Length of fabric for strap, according to your desired width and length. I used 48" x 2.75", which results in a thin strap of about 1" wide. Again, it is best to use a heavily woven fabric for strength. If you wish to use a lightweight fabric, it is recommended that you reinforce it with some iron-on interfacing before sewing.
- Fabric for pocket. 9.5" x 13.5".
- About 7" of 3/4" bias binding. Alternatively, make your own binding to match the fabric used inside bag.

Step One

Cut 6 pieces of fabric as specified in materials list.

Step Two

Fold pocket fabric in half on long edge with right sides facing, making a rectangle of approximately 9.5" wide x 6.75" high.

Step Three

Sew up the 2 short sides of pocket, turn inside out and press.

Step Four

Run a gathering seam approximately 1/2" below unsewn long edge (top of pocket). Pull threads to gather fabric until you reach your desired size for pocket opening (4.5" here).

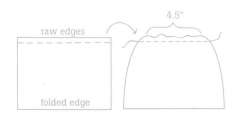

Step Five

Pin binding into place on top of pocket and sew in, leaving approximately 1/2" at each end. Remove gathering threads.

Step Six

Pin pocket to piece of fabric that you will use for the front (outside) of your bag, tucking binding edges under to produce a neat edge at top of pocket. This will make a self-lined pocket. Sew into place along three edges & put aside.

Step Seven

Press strap fabric as shown – folding strap in half lengthwise, and folding edges in a further 1/6" as you iron. Sew this length together along long edge, as close to edge as possible. Put aside.

Step Eight

With your two pieces of cut fabric facing right sides together, sew bag lining along the two long edges and one short edge – leaving a hole of about 4" in the latter. The remaining open edge will be the top opening of your bag. Turn right side out.

Step Nine

Place pieces of fabric to be used for outside of bag right sides together (making sure pocket is facing right side-up!), and sew along same edges as in Step Eight. This time do not leave a hole in the short edge.

Step Ten

Leaving outside of bag inside out, place sewn strap inside bag and pin ends into place at the unsewn top of the bag on the side seams. Remember to ensure your strap is not twisted to allow for a neat, comfortable drape.

strap ends (pin in place)

outer bag (wrong side)

Step Eleven

Place the bag lining (still turned right side out) inside the bag so that the two right sides are facing with the strap sandwiched in between. Pin both layers together along top (open) edge. Sew along top perimeter to secure bag, lining and strap.

lining (wrong side)

outside fabric (wrong side)

Step Thirteen

Turn inside out through hole in bottom of lining.

Step Fourteen

Press bag, paying special attention to top perimeter. Run another seam along the top edge. This will leave you with a professional finish and give extra strength and security to the strap.

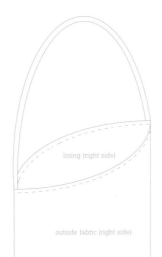

lining (right side)

outside fabric (right side)

Step Fifteen

Sew up hole in the lining of your bag and embellish your tote as desired. Pop your library card in the pocket and load her up with books!

These are the circle templates for the Flower Brooch. Instructions are on page 134.

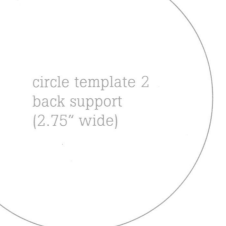

circle template 1
back flower piece
(3.5" wide)

circle template 2
back support
(2.75" wide)

Tissue Cover

Materials

- 1/4 yards of various prints, preferably of a medium to heavy weight cotton. You can mix and match patterns for each piece of the house.
- Black felt and white felt for the eyes
- Embroidery floss

Step One

Cut the following pieces:
- House Sides: 5.25" x 5.25" (x 4 from outside fabric, x 4 from inside fabric)
- Roof Sides: 5.25" x 4.5" (x 2 from outside roof fabric, x 2 from inside fabric) (See Pattern for Chimney Hole)
- Chimney: 1.75" x 4.75" (x 4)
- Roof Triangle: See Pattern Pieces (x 2 of outer fabric, x 2 of inner fabric)
- Eyes: See Pattern Pieces (x 2 of smaller, x 2 of larger)

All measurements include 1/4" seam allowance.

Step Two

Take chimney pieces and sew all four together along the long edges, right sides together.

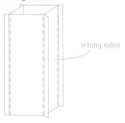

Step Three

Next turn the chimney right-side-out and then tuck half of the chimney inside itself.

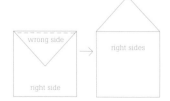

Step Four

Take the two roof side pieces (cut from the outside fabric) and place them right-sides-together. Sew along one of the 5.25" sides. Repeat with the inside roof pieces.

Step Five

Sew triangles to two of the outside house sides. Repeat with two of the inside house sides.

Step Six

Sew triangle house parts to the roof sides. Repeat for inside pieces.

Step Seven

Then sew the last sides on all the house parts. Repeat for inside pieces.

Step Eight

Now you will have two houses, one made from inner fabrics, one from outer.

Step Nine

Now you want to sandwich the houses so the right sides of the fabric are facing each other. It doesn't matter which house is on the outside, just make sure to line up all the house parts so they fit together nicely.

Step Ten

With your sewing machine, sew along the bottom edges leaving one side open. This is so you can turn the houses right side out. Make careful note when sewing to line up all the corners on the house.

Step Eleven

Next turn the house right side out, and carefully sew along the edge to keep the house from curling. When you get to the side that was not sewn, just tuck the ends in and sew it closed.

Step Twelve

Line up the square opening for the chimney in the roof.

Step Thirteen

Working one side at a time, hand stitch the chimney to the outer side of the house. Use small neat stitches and a thread color that will blend in with your fabric. If you find your hole too small, it's okay. You can carefully tuck the fabric a little as you go along. You do not want the hole to be too big.

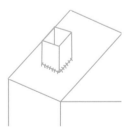

Step Fourteen

Turn the house wrong side out, and finish stitching the

chimney on this side. If you can see the stitches more on this side, it won't matter. They will be inside and not be seen once the house is complete.

Step Fifteen
Lastly turn the house right sides out again and choose which side you'd like the face on.

Step Sixteen
Using red embroidery thread, backstitch a mouth. You can hide your end knots

where the eyes will go. Make sure you are only stitching through the top layer of fabric, so the stitches won't show on the underside

Step Seventeen
Use fabric glue to glue eyes over the end knots.

Step Eighteen
Once completely dry pull house over tissue box. Use one hand to pull the first tissue up through the chimney to look like smoke. Be careful not to pull the tissue out too far.

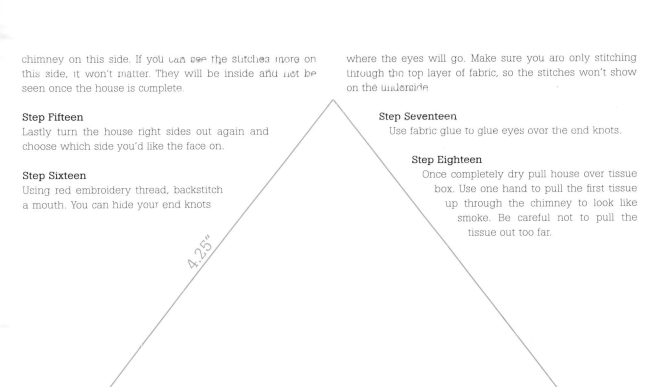

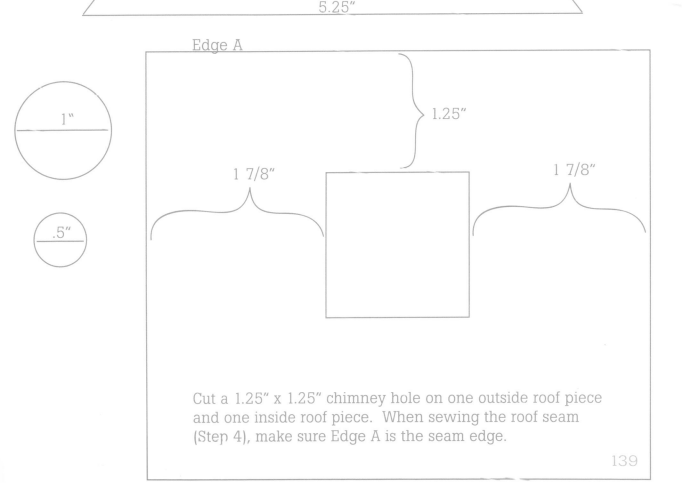

Edge A

1"

.5"

1.25"

1 7/8"

1 7/8"

Cut a 1.25" x 1.25" chimney hole on one outside roof piece and one inside roof piece. When sewing the roof seam (Step 4), make sure Edge A is the seam edge.

139

Pillowcase Apron

Materials

- 1 thrifted pillowcase
- 1 package of twill tape
- Fabric pen/pencil

Step One

Wash the pillowcase, iron it, and fold it in half, with the opening facing the bottom.

Step Two

Lay out the supplies you want to carry with you in your apron and mark the size and placement of the pockets you'd like. Use your fabric pen or pencil to draw the pocket on the apron.

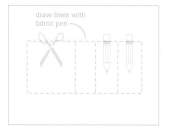

Step Three

To make the openings for the pockets, unfold the pillowcase, and sew through just the two layers using the zigzag stitch, essentially making a giant button hole the size of each pocket opening that you've marked out. Use scissors or a rotary cutter to very carefully cut open the 'buttonhole.'

Step Four

Lay the apron back down folded over on itself and pin through all 4 layers to keep it in place. Sew along the lines you've marked out to be the pockets. Also sew right along the top of the zigzagged buttonhole to anchor down the top layer to the bottom.

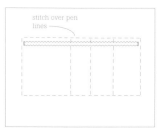

Step Five

Measure pieces of twill tape long enough to either tie nicely in back, or super long to wrap all the way around and tie in front. Lay the apron down flat and fold over a pleat on either side of the waistband. Stick the ends of your two pieces of twill tape in there, pin and sew into place. You can make the pleats as near the middle or edges as you'd like, or you can skip pleats altogether and sew the twill tape on at the edges.

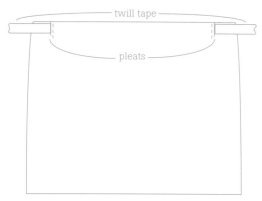

Step Six

Send the apron through the wash to get out fabric pen/pencil, and you're all set!

Ice Cream
Pin Cushion

Materials

Miniature flower pot (1" x 1 1/8")
- 1/4 yard of Fabric A
- 1/4 yard of Fabric B
- 1 quilter's pin (with pink pinhead)
- 1 medium sized red bead
- Fabric glue

Step One
Trace circle template on fabric A. Cut out circle.

Step Two
Using needle and thread make a running stitch (pass the needle over and under the fabric) just inside the circle's edge, leaving about a centimeter between your stitching and the edge of the circle. Continue stitching around the entire circle.

Step Three
Once you've stitched around the entire circle, pull gently on your thread to slightly cinch up the circle so that it forms the shape of a bowl.

Step Four
Fill the cinched circle with stuffing, and cinch the circle tighter until it's closed, forming a puff.

Step Five
Holding the circle closed, pull the thread taut and knot it to close up the circle, making sure not to let any stuffing get out.

Step Six
Repeat steps 1–5 for fabric B.

Step Seven
To form the two scoops of ice-cream: Stack puff A on top of puff B.

Step Eight
Using needle and thread, connect puff A to puff B: Sew A to the top of B using small stitches from bottom of puff A through top of puff B.

Step Nine
Once both puffs are secured together, fill the inside of your flower pot with glue and gently set the ice cream into the pot, making sure to tuck the sides of puff B into pot's upper rim.

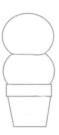

Step Ten
To make cherry on top: Place pink pin into hole of red bead. Stick pin into ice cream.

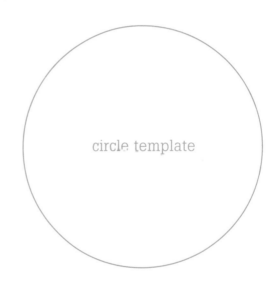

circle template

Pebble Bracelet

Materials

- 1 hank of merino tops for felting in colour of your choice
- Two 12" pieces of .8mm diameter beading elastic, clear
- 10 beads for spacers (mine are about 5mm) with holes big enough to fit elastic
- Scraps of silk in five colours, preferably Shantung with a different coloured warp and weft (cut into 1" square pieces)
- Super glue
- Baby shampoo or soap
- Gold thread

Tools

- Sewing needle to fit gold thread
- Darning needle to fit elastic
- Bradawl or other pointy instrument for making holes in beads
- Scissors
- Pot of boiling or very hot water
- Pot of cold water
- Slotted spoon
- Tea towels

Step One

Cut 4" lengths of wool from your tops. Separate these lengths into half width-wise and then spread out five of them on your work surface. Open up the lengths of the wool fibre, to prepare for felting.

Step Two

layer one

Lay one group so that the length of the fibres runs vertically and then lay a second group of fibres over top, with the fibres running horizontally.

Step Three

Lay a third group of fibres vertically, the fourth horizontally, and the fifth and final group vertically. You should now have a stack of five lengths of wool top. Sprinkle a bit of hot, soapy water solution on top of the wool fibres.

Step Four

Begin to gently roll this group of fibres into a ball between your hands, as you might with play dough. Do not apply much pressure. Gently does it at this stage.

Step Five

The wool should "stick" together quite easily because of all the soap. Keep rolling; if it refuses to come together, add a little more soapy water, but not so much that it is soaking and unmanageable.

Step Six

cover a fissure with extra wool

If you keep rolling gently, it should come into a nice neat ball with no cracks or fissures. If a crack does seem to appear then take a few wisps of merino and lay them over the cracked area; use lots of soap on your hands to "stick" them in place. Keep rolling gently and the crack area should get hidden nicely. As long as you don't apply too much pressure, you can keep adding wool to the ball in this way.

Step Seven

At this stage you could complete the felt bead by just rolling more and more vigorously until all the fibres are completely felted into a hard ball. But for this project we are going to do something a bit different.

Firstly, we want the beads to be more of a button shape so they fit nicely against the wrist. Press the top of your bead down with the flat of your palm as much as you can.

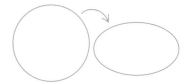

Step Eight

Now we are going to add the silk scraps. There are ways of adding fabric bits to felt with no sewing but this method uses a needle and thread, and also shapes the bead at the same time.

silk scrap (with stitch)

anchoring stitches

I have used a gold thread so that where it shows you get a glint of metallic. Anchor your needle and thread in the felt bead with a few stitches and then bring the needle up through the bead and a square of silk. Bring the needle back down through the silk, catching in an end and then come out through the other side of the bead. Continue adding scraps of silk in the same way.

Step Nine

The idea is to pull the needle through the felt so that it continues to form an oval bead shape and attach the silk squares. I've sewn through each of the silk scraps two or three times, catching a different area each time.

The result is the silk gets pulled into the felt slightly. The silk will have lots of shaggy threads hanging off but they shouldn't shed too much because they have been caught up in the stitches.

While you are working on the bead the silk will get wet and change colour. The beads will be more vibrant and contrasty when they dry. My beads are about 4–5cm in diameter and include about 15 pieces of silk.

Step Ten

Make 5 large beads in this way. When they are done put them in the hot water, swish them around and press them down with the slotted spoon to get all the soap out of the felt and then transfer them to the cold water to shock the wool.
Squeeze the beads out between to towels to get all the water out and reshape them. Let dry.

Step Eleven

To string the beads, have your bradawl, darning needle, and two pieces of elastic, spacer beads, bulldog clips, and pliers ready.
Begin by making a channel for the elastic in the beads with the bradawl. You can only make one channel at a time because they will close up after a few seconds.

Step Twelve

With the elastic threaded through the darning needle, push the needle through the threading channel. Sometimes it's helpful to have a pair of pliers to pull the needle through.

Snap the bulldog clip on to one end of the elastic so that it doesn't pull through the bead as you thread the bracelet.

Step Thirteen

I have used two spacer beads, about 2cm apart, between each felt bead. I poked a second channel and threaded the elastic through. You may then need to take the needle off the elastic so that you can thread the spacer beads. Repeat this process until you have all 5 felt beads and the spacers between each threaded onto the elastics.

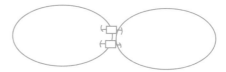

Test the bracelet to see if it fits nicely and then tie the elastic ends to their beginnings with a double or triple knot. Make sure the knots are secure, by putting a drop of super glue on each.

Rethread the elastic ends onto your darning needle and use your pair of pliers to pull the knots to the inside of a felt bead. Trim the elastic ends.

Log Cabin Pillow

Materials
- fabric (1/4 yards of several different prints
- 1/2 yard of cotton batting
- 1/4 of pre-quilted fabric for back
- small length of ribbon

Step One
Select your fabrics. These can either be ten-fifteen different prints to avoid repeats, or a selection of five or six prints which coordinate. The fewer fabrics you use, the more carefully you'll have to arrange them to avoid placing matching prints next to each other.

Step Two
Using a rotary cutter and transparent ruler, cut 1.5-2.5" strips. The length of the strips will vary. You can trim off any extra length after sewing a strip on, and you can patch together two shorter strips to get the required length. Depending on the width of your strips, you'll need around 20-25.

Step Three
Start with center square, which should be 2.5" x 2.5". Begin building outward following this pattern:

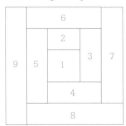

Begin by sewing piece 1 to piece 2. Iron the seam flat, trim the edges to be square, and then sew on piece 3. Continue ironing the seams, trimming, and adding the next piece.

Step Four
Continue building in this way until the patchwork is the size you need (if you don't have another cushion cover to work from, measure your pillow insert from one side to the other, taking into account the curve, and add an extra inch for good measure). To vary the look of your patchwork, you can use the trimmed off ends from previous strips and patch them end to end to make new strips.

Step Five
Once the quilt square is the size you'd like, lay it down on cotton batting (a piece larger than the quilt square) on a flat surface and pin the quilt square to the batting.

Step Six
Trim the batting about an inch larger than the quilt square

Step Seven
Begin machine quilting the square to the batting starting from the inside and sew out from the inside, continuously turning at each corner

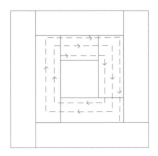

Step Eight
Once it's all quilted, trim the batting flush with the edge of the patchwork piece.

Step Nine
To make the back, cut two pieces from the pre-quilted fabric. Each piece should be as wide as your patchwork top. To determine the length of your piece, halve the width of your patchwork top and add three inches.

Step Ten
Take one of the pieces and fold down the wide end by 2", and zig zag this down using a contrasting thread. Repeat with the other piece.

width of patchwork

Step Ten
Turn the two back pieces over, so the turned-over edge is facing down. You're now looking at the right side. Sew a 10" length of ribbon to the middle of each piece.

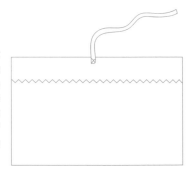

Step Eleven

To finish the piece, take your patchwork and lay it flat, right-side-up. Take one of the back pieces and lay it on top of the patchwork. It should be right-side-down, with the folded-over edge towards the middle, like so:

The bottom corners should all match up. Lay down the other back piece in the same way, but with the top corners matching. The two back pieces should overlap in the middle by at least 1". Pin this all in place.

Step Twelve

Sew around all four side, leaving a 1/4" seam.

Step Thirteen

Remove the pins and turn the pillow cover right-side-out through the opening of the two back pieces.

Step Fourteen

Squeeze your pillow insert into the case through the back opening and tie the two ribbons in a bow to finish.

These are the templates for the Corsage. Instructions are on page 135.

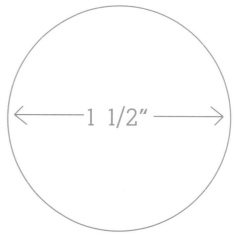

Desk Organizer

Materials
- 1/2 meter of thick felt
- fabric glue
- embroidery thread and sharp needle
- fusible fabric for backing
- thin tape (optional)

Step One
Cut a piece of graph paper to the size you'd like the box to be, for example, the size of the drawer of your sewing table.

Step Two
Arrange the objects you want to organize on the graph paper. Draw lines to mark off the sections. You can also annotate this sheet with what goes where, color choices, etc.

Step Three
Cut a piece of felt the size of the graph paper. A rotary cutter and a gridded cutting mat are the best tools for this.

Step Four
Cut strips of felt for the walls and dividers. Lower walls work better or else they get floppy. I used 1.75" tall walls. Leave extra length so you can cut the strips to the exact size while assembling.

Step Five
Mark the sections on the felt. I used quilter's tape, which comes in convenient widths and comes off easily. You could use any thin tape or draw the lines on. The tape is nice because it helps

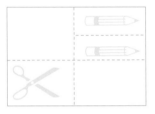

you account for the thickness of the walls in framing the embroidery.

Step Six
Choose a color scheme of embroidery threads. A narrow selection of colors can help unify the project. I picked out 4 bright colors plus grey and dark brown.

Step Seven
Embroider each section with the object that will go in it. A sharp needle works better on the thick felt than a standard dull embroidery needle. Use 1 or 2 strands of the 6-stranded floss, knotted at the end. You can do the pictures freehand, or by making a drawing to follow. You can also "trace" an object by anchoring it with a few stitches and embroidering around for an outline. For the text, you might find it helpful to choose a font you like and print out templates. I used basic embroidery stitches: backstitch/straight stitch (text, most outlines), couching (knitting needles, pins, thread from bobbins), satin stitch (bobbins), daisy stitch (scallops on red button), and French knots (pin heads, dots on i's, button holes).

Step Eight
Remove the tape marking the sections.

Step Nine
To keep the thread ends secure, fuse a piece of fabric to the backs of the embroidered pieces. Trim excess fabric.

Step Ten
Starting with the two short outer walls of the box, trim to the exact size of the embroidered base. Run a bead of glue along the bottom of each strip. Arrange flush and hold until set. Wipe off any excess glue with a damp cloth.

Step Eleven
Cut the two long outer walls to the correct size, accounting for the space taken up by the already glued walls. Run a bead of glue along the bottom and both ends of each strip. Set in place, pinching the joints to secure.

Step Twelve
Once the outer walls are set, use the same method to glue in the dividers.

Step Thirteen
Let glue cure completely before using.

For Machine Embroidery
- Work as above, except use thinner felt for the bottom. The thick felt is trickier to use with a machine.
- Any sewing machine will work for machine embroidery. First, drop the feed dogs and remove the normal foot. Using a darning/free motion foot helps but is not necessary. (If you go foot-less, watch your fingers!) Thread it up with any color in the bobbin thread and the desired color as the top thread. Test the tension first on a scrap of felt and adjust so you can't see the bobbin thread on the top, but it's not all loopy on the back. Keeping the fabric flat against the machine, move it in a smooth motion under the needle to make the drawing. If you need to move to another place in the drawing, simply pull the needle up and move there. The connecting threads will all be trimmed at the end.
- Using a small pair of scissors, trim all the connecting threads.
- Finish as above.

Backstitch

Satin Stitch

Couching Stitch

Daisy Stitch
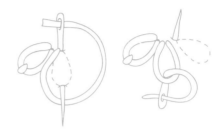

French Knot

Summer Top

Materials

- T-shirt (see instructions below)
- 1 yard of fabric
- Pins
- Tailor's chalk or equivalent

Step One

Find a T-shirt or tank top that has a fit you adore. You will be using the shirt (hereafterS referred to as the "pattern shirt") to make your pattern, so make sure that it is not too snug or fitted, as you will need some room to get the summer top over your head! Don't worry about cutting the shirt – that won't happen if you are careful.

Step Two

Put on the pattern shirt. With a pin, mark where you would like the top of the summer top to sit. If you would like the length of the top to be different than the pattern shirt, take another pin and mark where you'd like the bottom of the top to be. Determine the placement of the straps. A good spot is about an inch in from your armpit. Take a

pin and mark where you want the outer edge of the strap to hit. Do this on both sides.

Step Three

Place your fabric on a cutting surface. The fabric should be folded in half, with the selvedges on the sides. Carefully place your T-shirt on top of the fabric, with the top of the shirt even with one of the cut edges. Make sure the shirt is centered on the fabric. Using the tailor's chalk, mark 2" below where you want the bottom of the shirt to be (this will give you a 2" hem allowance). Cut along the marked line.

Step Four

Fold the pattern shirt down to where the pin is that marks the top of the shirt. With your tailor's chalk, mark 1/2"

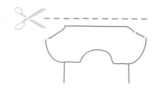

above the top of the pattern shirt. Cut along the marked line.

Step Five

Next you want to determine the center line of the pattern shirt. Carefully lift up the right or left side of the pattern shirt and fold it in half lengthwise, so the left side meets the right. Place pins on the fabric you're cutting to mark this center line. Mark 1/2" beyond the side of the pattern shirt with your tailor's chalk. Things get a little tricky when you get to the armhole, but don't panic. Basically, you want to cut a curve along the armhole, ending at the outer edge of where the straps will be. Good thing you have already marked that spot! Using that trusty tailor's chalk, mark 1/2" beyond the curve of the pattern shirt's armhole. You'll need to lift up the sleeve of the pattern shirt as you go to see the armhole seam. Get the pattern

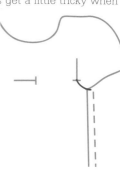

shirt out of the way and cut along the marked line. Fold your fabric along the pinned center line and cut the other side of the shirt to match.

Step Six

You're nearly there! Now you want to cut the facing. Place a piece of folded fabric underneath the top of the cut shirt, lining up the top edges. The fabric should be long enough that it extends about 2-3" below the bottom of the armhole. Mark and cut along the armholes. The bottom of the facing should also be even and straight, so do a little cutting if necessary.

Step Seven

You only have the straps left to cut. If you plan on using ribbon or something else, you can skip this step and get right to sewing! You need to determine how long you want the straps to be. It's okay if you cut them too long. Take a straight edge and place it along the pin on the pattern shirt that marks where you want the top of the shirt to be. Measure from the straight edge to the top of the shoulder on the pattern shirt. Double this amount then add 1" for good measure. Let's call this measurement S for now. You are going to cut two strips of fabric: measurement S long by 4 1/4" wide (this allows for a 1/2" seam allowance).

Step Eight

This is what all your pieces should look like.

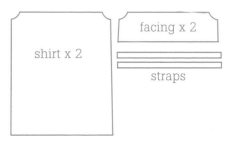

Step Nine

Let's get sewing! Let's do the straps first. Fold the straps in half lengthwise with right sides together. Pin and stitch along the long edge, using a 1/4" seam allowance. Turn the straps inside out and press flat with the seam in the middle of the strap (this is the part that will go against your shoulder so the seam will be invisible).

Step Ten

With right sides together, sew the outer sides of the facing (do NOT stitch the armholes). Press open the seams. Press the bottom of the facing under 1/2" for the hem. Stitch the hem, using a 3/8" seam allowance.

Step Eleven

Pin the front piece to the back piece with right sides together. Stitch down the side seams, using a 1/2" seam allowance. Press open the seams.

Step Twelve

Hem the top: fold up the bottom 1" to the inside and press. Fold again another inch and press. Pin and stitch down the hem, using a 1/4" seam allowance.

Step Thirteen

With right sides together, pin each strap to the front of the top. The edge of the straps should be in 1/2" from the upper edges of the top. Baste down the straps.

right side

Step Fourteen

Now you're going to attach the facing. Again with right sides together, pin the facing to the top, matching side seams and corners. Stitch all the way around (i.e., front and back and the armholes), using a 1/2" seam allowance.

wrong side

Step Fifteen

Take a pair of scissors and trim the seams down to about 3/8". Clip the curves and the corners. Turn the facing to the inside of the top and press carefully.

Step Sixteen

You're almost finished! Slip the top over your head. Oooh, hope it makes it. Have a friend pin the back straps to the desired length. Carefully remove the top. Make sure the back straps are pinned evenly and against the edges of the back, on the inside of the top. Pin around the top edge of the top. Topstitch all the way around for a clean look. Cut the excess off the back straps if necessary.

right side

Elephant Pouch

Materials

- 1/4 yard of outer fabric (grey)
- 1/4 yard of inner fabric (patterned)
- embroidery floss for face
- sew-on snap/press stud

Step One
Transfer patterns to fabric and cut out (see page 155 for continuation of pattern pieces). Line the fabric with interfacing to stabilize, if desired.

Step Two
Embroider eyes and mouth to the bottom half of the outer piece. A guide is printed on the pattern piece.

Step Three
Sew the trunk piece, clip around curves, and turn right-side-out. Stuff the trunk with fiberfill.

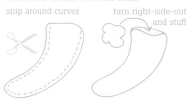

snip around curves   turn right-side-out and stuff

Step Four
Sew the top of the trunk closed and use floss to embroider lines along the trunk.

Step Five
Hand stitch the trunk to the outer fabric.

Step Six
Sew the two ear pieces. Clip along the curves and turn them right-side-out.

Step Seven
Position the ears on the face and baste into place about 1/8" from the edge.

Step Eight
Sew darts on pocket pieces, outer, and lining pieces, as marked on the pattern pieces.

Step Nine
With right sides together, sew the pocket pieces together along the top edge. Press along the right side of the pocket with an iron.

Step Ten
If you want your pouch to be slightly padded, cut a piece of batting the same size as the outer fabric piece. Clip where the darts would be located and position on the wrong side of the outer fabric piece.

Step Eleven
Line up the pocket piece with the outer lining piece and pin it in place. The grey (outer) side of the pocket piece will be face down on the outer fabric piece.

pocket piece (lining side up)

Step Twelve
Baste the pocket to the outer lining piece. Sew about 1/8" from the edge.

Step Thirteen
With right sides together, sew the outer fabric piece to the inner lining piece. Leave an opening at the bottom (the bottom part of the face) so that the piece can be turned right side out.

Step Fourteen
Turn right side out, through opening at the bottom of the face.

Step Fifteen
Flip the sewn pocket so that the lining fabric is on the inside of the pouch.

Step Sixteen
Slip-stitch the opening closed.

lining (the elephant face is on the other side of this)

pocket piece

Step Seventeen
Sew a snap onto the bottom of the pocket. Sew the other side of the snap to the top of the inner lining.

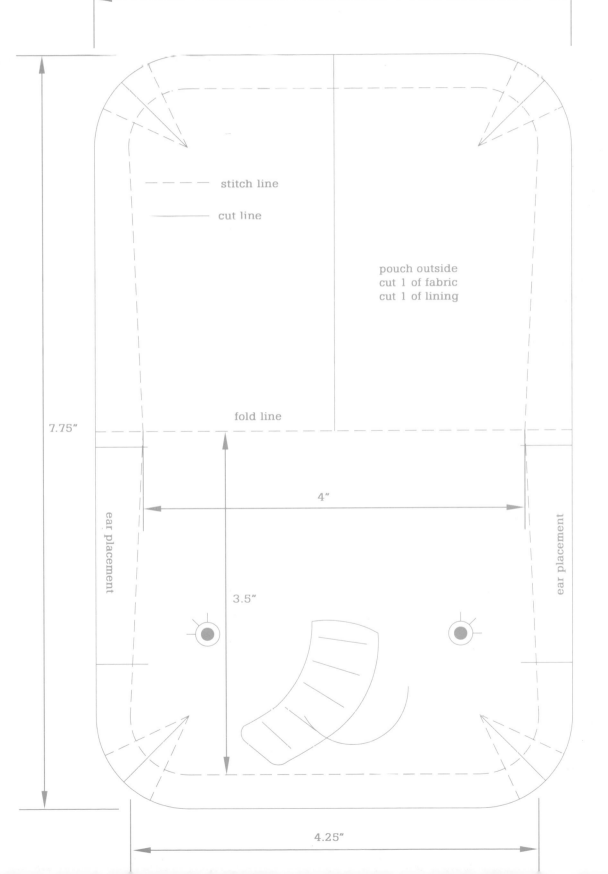

5"

stitch line

cut line

pouch outside
cut 1 of fabric
cut 1 of lining

fold line

7.75"

ear placement

ear placement

4"

3.5"

4.25"

Fabric Basket

Materials

- 1/2 yard, natural unbleached cotton canvas
- 1/2 yard, cotton lining fabric
- 1/2 yard, Pellon Tailors Touch Heavyweight Sew-in Stabilizer (or similar)
- 1/4 yard, Pellon Peltex Extra-Heavyweight Sew-in Stabilizer (or similar)
- 1 yard, Wrights Double Fold Extra Wide Bias Tape (Oyster 028)
- 1/3 yard, Wrights Double Fold Bias Tape (Oyster 028)
- 1 1/3 yard, Wrights 1/2" Wide Twill Tape (Oyster 028)
- 1 set of Sew On Velcro, about a 1 inch square piece, (white)

Step One

Cut out the following from your materials:

- 11" x 6.5" rectangle (front + back):
CUT 2 from natural unbleached canvas
CUT 2 from lining
CUT 2 from heavyweight stabilizer

- 5.25" x 6.5" rectangle (sides) :
CUT 2 from natural unbleached canvas
CUT 2 from heavyweight stabilizer

- 11" x 4" rectangle (pocket, cut on fold to result in a piece 11" x 8") * Place 11" side on fold for both materials:
CUT 2 from natural unbleached canvas
CUT 2 from heavyweight stabilizer

- 11" x 5.25" rectangle (bottom):
CUT 1 from natural unbleached canvas

- 10.5" x 4.75" rectangle (bottom, stabilizer):
CUT 1 from extra heavyweight stabilizer

- 6.5" x 24" rectangle (lining sides + bottom):
CUT 1 from cotton lining

- 3" x 10" rectangle (handles):
CUT 2 from natural unbleached canvas

- 17" x 7" rectangle (drawstring top):
CUT 2 from cotton lining

Step Two

Unless stated otherwise, all seam allowances are 1/4" (included in above measurements). The first step is to construct the pocket. Begin by opening up the folded pocket piece. On the 'wrong' side of the pocket, sew in your Velcro closure in the middle of the

pocket and about ½" from the folded edge. You will only sew down this side of the Velcro right now.

Insert the stabilizer in between your canvas pocket front so that both folds match up at the top. Baste stitch top edge at fold. Sew on the Wrights Double Fold Bias Tape to the top edge (at fold) of the pocket.

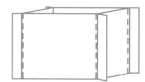

Lay down your basket front on top of a matching piece of stabilizer. Baste one side of the pocket down to the basket front and basket front stabilizer.

At this point, you can stitch in the other side of your velcro closure to the basket front, making sure the front and back piece line up. Sew the remaining piece just underneath the pocket front on the right side of the basket front.

Step Three

Sew the sides of the basket together. Starting with the basket front, begin sewing together the sides of the basket together, right sides together. Do not forget to include the stabilizer to the back of each canvas piece. Continue sewing up each side until you have a long strip of basket side, basket back, basket side and basket front. Next, stitch together the basket front to the remaining basket side.

Step Four

Make basket handles. To construct the basket handles, fold in and press each edge by 1/2" and then fold the strip in half. Topstitch around the edges of the handle.

Sew the handles to the sides of the basket, 1/2" inch from the top and sides. Sew a 1" square on the handle and then stitch an X through the center to ensure it's not going anywhere.

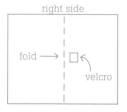

Step Five

Construct basket bottom. The first step to making the basket bottom is to sew down the extra-heavy weight stabilizer to the wrong side of the basket bottom. To do this, center the Peltex on the basket bottom and stitch around the edges.

Next pin the basket bottom in place around the bottom edges of the basket, right sides together. Sew together.

Turn right-side-out. You now have a basket shape that is wonderfully stable and ready to be lined.

Step Six

Sew basket lining. To construct the basket liner, first sew down the front and back piece, right sides together, to the middle of the basket bottom/side piece, as shown below.

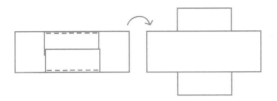

Next, pin and sew up the sides of the lining to construct the basket shape.

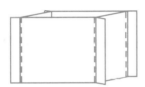

Place lining in basket, wrong sides together, and pin in place. Baste stitch around the top of the basket as close to the edge as possible, trim seam.

Step Seven

Construct drawstring top. To make the drawstring top of the basket, first make the casing for the twill tape. Measure 1.5" in from both sides, 3" down on both ends, mark with a pencil. The 3" space at the top will become your twill tape casing. At the mark you just made, make a 1.5" long cut, 3" down from the top on both ends. Repeat for the top back. Fold over this small rectangular piece on to the wrong side of the top and sew down at the folded edge.

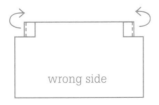

wrong side

Fold over the casing into thirds and stitch along the bottom. Repeat for the other side.

Wirh right sides together, sew up the sides of your drawstring top, 1.5" in from the sides to line up the edge of the drawstring pocket. Trim seam.

wrong side

Attach one end of your twill tape to a safety pin and carefully thread it through the casing, turning and going through the other side, so the ends meet where you started. Knot both ends of your twill tape together and trim excess.

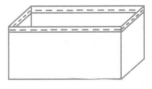

Pull knotted end through casing top until you have loops on either end. This will hide the devilishly ugly knot.

Step Eight

Pin the drawstring top to the basket by lining up the raw edge of drawstring top with the top basted edge of the basket. Pin wrong side of drawstring top to right side of basket lining. Pin and sew in place.

Step Nine

The last step is to pin the Wrights Double Fold Extra Wide Bias Tape onto the top edge of the basket. Sew around the top edge, folding under the bias tape where the beginning and end meets.

Book Cover

The measurements in these instructions are for a book cover identical to the one pictured (which measures 4.25" x 6.75"). If your books are a different size, use their measurements, plus 1/4" for 'comfort' (and don't forget your 1/4" seam allowance!).

Materials

- 1/4 yard of printed fabric for book cover exterior (1)
- large scrap of solid matching fabric for binding section and velcro flap (2)
- 1/4 yard of solid fabric for book cover interior (3)
- Velcro

Step One

Cut your pieces out (measurements here include a 1/4" seam allowance).
- Piece A (7.5" x 10"): Cut 1 from the exterior fabric (1), cut 1 from interior fabric (3).
- Piece B (7.5" x 5.25"): Cut 2 from interior fabric (3).
- Piece C (3" x 1.75"): Cut 2 from solid fabric (2).
- Piece D (2" x 7.5"): Cut 1 from solid fabric (2).

Step Two

On piece A, trace a line at the top and bottom seam allowances to mark the center of the piece.

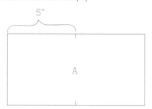

On piece D, mark the center line and draw the seam allowance line on the long sides (on the wrong side).

Step Three

Fold over and press the sides of piece D on the seam allowance line, and baste them in place. Pin it to the cover exterior, using the center markings as a guideline. Machine stitch up both sides, attaching piece D to A. Remove the basting stitches from D.

Step Four

With right sides together, machine stitch both pieces of the flap (C) together, leaving one of the smaller side open. Clip the bottom corners and turn it right-side-out.

Step Five

With the cover exterior right side up, pin the flap to the center of one side of the cover exterior. The finished edge should be in the center.

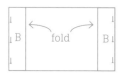

Take both Piece Bs and fold them in half lengthwise. Pin these to each side of the exterior fabric, making sure the folded part lies to the center.

Finally, pin the inside fabric on top of the other pieces, right-side-down.

Step Six

Sew around all four sides, leaving a 3" hole at the bottom center, to turn your cover. Clip the corners and turn right-side-out.

Slip stitch the turning hole closed.

Step Seven

Cut two small pieces of velcro and backstitch one to the underside of the flap and the other to the book cover. Make sure to only catch one layer of fabric when you sew them on, so you won't see the stitches on the other side.

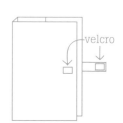

Your book cover is now finished!

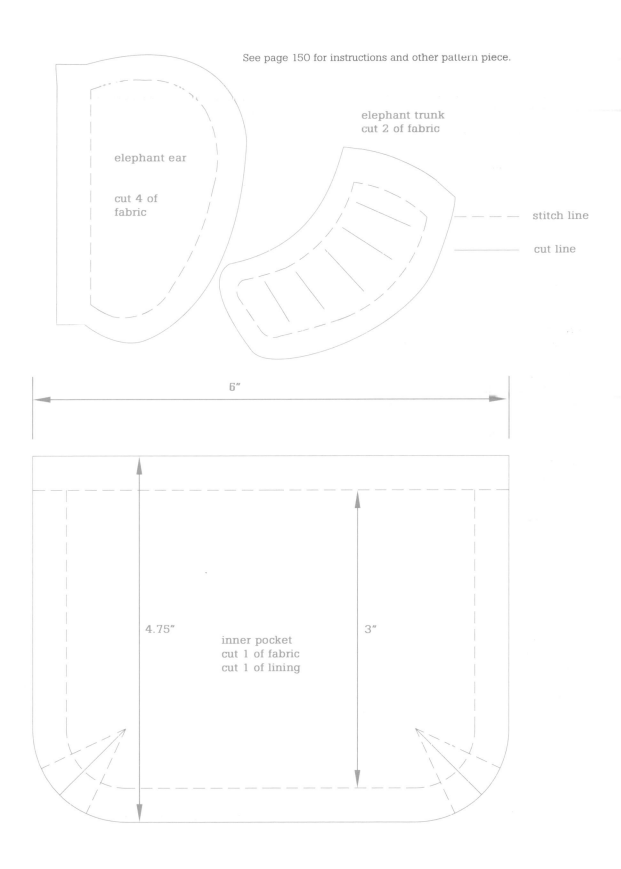

See page 150 for instructions and other pattern piece.

elephant trunk
cut 2 of fabric

elephant ear

cut 4 of
fabric

stitch line

cut line

6"

4.75"

3"

inner pocket
cut 1 of fabric
cut 1 of lining

Needle Case

Materials

- Piece 1 – 18" x 18" (outside piece)
- Piece 2 – 18" x 18" (inside piece)
- Piece 3 – 18" x 26" (pocket for needles)
- Piece 4 – 18" x 18" (inner flap to protect needle)
- 24" of ribbon or twill tape

Step One

Piece 4 – Start with the flap that keeps the needles from falling out. Fold it in half, right sides together, so it measures 18" x 9". Iron flat and sew a seam all the way around, leaving a small opening to turn piece inside out. After sewing seam, turn inside out and iron flat.

Step Two

Tuck in opening and close, then sew another seam all around on right side to close hole and flatten all edges.

Step Three

Piece 3 – Fold this piece in half, right sides out, to measure 18" x 13".

With the fold at the top, take a ruler and measure 5" down one of the 13 inch sides and mark. Place one end of your ruler at 5" mark and the other end at top corner of other 13" side. Cut a diagonal line from top corner to 5" mark. Save cut off piece.

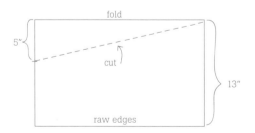

Step Four

Place Piece 3 right sides together with diagonal edges lined up and sew all around four sides, leaving a small opening to turn inside out.

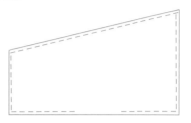

Step Five

Iron flat once turned inside out. Tuck in open hole and sew again around four edges to close and flatten all edges, as you did in Step Two.

Step Six

Take a ruler and determine where you want all the little pockets to be for your needles. Mark these lines with tailor's chalk. Make some big and some small. You can make one big enough to keep scissors or pencils as well. Lay this piece (Piece 3) right side up onto Piece 2 (also right side up), and sew down the lines you drew, thus attaching the two together.

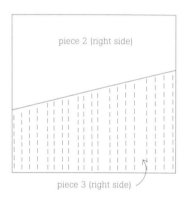

Step Seven

Take the cut off triangle from Step 3 and turn it right sides together. Sew edges closed, leaving hole to turn inside out. Turn and push the point out carefully. Iron flat, stitch around the edges and line up flat edge with flat edge of piece 4 – the flap. Sew in along joining edge.

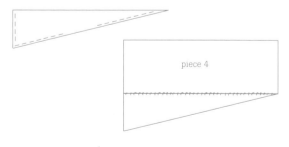

Step Eight

Body of case – Place Piece 1 (outside piece) and Piece 2 (inside piece) right sides together and sew all around, leaving a small opening to turn inside out. Do so, and iron flat.
Tuck in opening and sew a seam again, all around edges, to close hole and flatten piece.

Step Nine

Sew top edge of the needle protector flap to top edge of body.

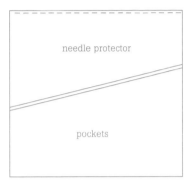

needle protector

pockets

Step Ten

Fill your case with needles and roll it up. Make a mark on the roll where you're going to sew your ribbon. It should be on the opposite side of the roll as the opening.

make mark here, halfway
down the length of the case

Step Eleven

Find the middle of your ribbon or twill tape and hand sew this in place over the mark. Now when you roll up your case, you can bring the ribbon around to the front and tie it in a bow to secure the roll.

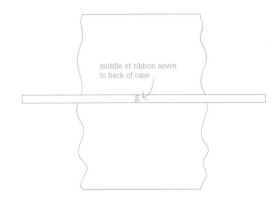

middle of ribbon sewn
to back of case

Starting Your Own Blog

Join In!

So you want to join us on the web, eh? As you can tell, everybody in this book loves keeping a blog, both as an outlet for their thoughts as well as a sort of showcase for their work. And most of all, we love finding new blogs to add to our daily reads!

If you've never set up a website before, your best bet is probably one of the many on-line journal websites, where you can simply join up and start blogging. A few of the most popular of these sites are Blogger (http://www.blogger.com/), Livejournal (http://www.livejournal.com/), Typepad (http://www.typepad.com/), and Wordpress (http://www.wordpress.com/)

Blogger, Livejournal, and Wordpress are all free to join, and Typepad has a monthly fee depending on the level of service and functionality you want. Many people are now switching to Typepad, the newest of the four, despite the fee, as some of their features are unique to their service.

Once you've chosen and join up, there are a few things to think about regarding your content and design. Chances are you'll be using a ready-made template for your blog, but that doesn't really have to determine the look or popularity of your site (not that this is a popularity contest!). These are my tips:

Use Photos

Lots of photos! As crafters, we're all quite visual people, and we want to see what you've been up to. It might not be fair, but you'll probably find it much more difficult to hook new readers if they're presented with block after block of text and no images. Sites like Flickr (http://www.flickr.com/) are making it very easy to upload your photos to share with the world, so don't be hesitant! You don't have to post pictures of yourself or your family, but if you're describing the new tea cosy you've made, by all means, show it to us from every angle!

Link Your Way to Fame

You might think that having a list of links on your blog would send people away, and we don't want that. But actually, links can say a lot about a person. If your links are like mine, it turns out we like the same people and probably have the same tastes. If they're not, hooray! – New blogs to check out. Even more importantly, links can get you noticed by the people you're linking to. If they see you've linked to them, they're much more likely to check out your blog and link back to you (though this isn't guaranteed!). Links also place your blog within the network; without them, you're floating out there on your own.

Comment!

An even more immediate way to get noticed is to comment on other blogs. We're all a little bit nervous to share ourselves with the world, so when somebody leaves a glowing comment, we're delighted and interested to know who left it. Make sure you fill in your name and web address when leaving a comment, and you can be almost positive that the blogger will visit your site, even if they don't make their presence known.

Opening comments on your own blog can be nerve-wracking. There are so many things to worry about – Will people leave hurtful comments? Will they leave no comments? Does that mean they don't like me? Don't they even know I'm out here? It probably is true that you'll have only a few comments when you first get going, but stick with it. You're the only person who's going to promote your blog, so get out there and do it – not overtly, because nobody wants to hear people saying, 'Look at my new website! Look!' – but by leaving comments for others and linking to them. If you're supportive of others, they'll want to support you too, you can almost count on it. The community of crafty bloggers is built upon our desire to share and support each other, and there's always room for more!

Resources

Yarn

UK

Get Knitted (www.getknitted.com)

Hip Knits (www.hipknits.co.uk)

Loop (www.loop.gb.com)

Texere Yarns (www.texere.co.uk)

US

Handpaintedyarn – (www.handpaintedyarn.com)

Australia

Martas Yarns – (www.martasyarns.com.au)

Fabric and Notions

UK

Antique Angel (www.antiqueangel.co.uk)

Cotton Patch (www.cottonpatch.net)

Earthenwood Studios (www.earthenwoodstudio.com)

Kitty Craft (www.kitty-craft.com)

Kleins (www.kleins.co.uk)

Liberty (Regent Street, London)

Stitch in Time (www.stitchintimeuk.com)

US

Cias Palette (www.ciaspalette.com)

Cloth Doll Supply (www.clothdollsupply.com)

Dharma Trading (www.dharmatrading.com)

Fat Quarter Shop (www.fatquartershop.com)

Twining Thread (www.twiningthread.com)

Reprodepot Fabrics (www.reprodepotfabrics.com)

Weir Dolls (www.weirdolls.com)

Australia

Prints Charming – (www.printscharming.com.au)

Handmade Shops

Buy Olympia (www.buyolympia.com)

Cut + Paste (www.cutxpaste.com)

Fred Flare (www.fredflare.com)

Lemon Maid (www.lemonademaid.com)

Plain Mabel (www.plainmabel.com)

These links are accurate as of the printing of this book. Please let us know of any changes by e-mailing Snowbooks at crafterscompanion@snowbooks.com.

Acknowledgements

I'd like to offer huge thanks to everybody who contributed to this book and everybody who supported us along the way. None of us would be creating and crafting the way we do if it weren't for those special people in our lives.

My personal thanks go to Cara Rodway, who was an enthusiastic model for many of the photos in this book. And thank you to everybody (including my mother!) who looked over the patterns and made sure we got everything right.